Lost Lands
and
Sunken Cities

Nigel Pennick

Lost Lands and Sunken Cities

©1997 Nigel Pennick

ISBN 1 898307 83 0

Original edition published 1987
Updates and revised edition published 1997

ALL RIGHTS RESERVED

No part of this publication may be reproduced, stored in a retrieval system or transmitted in any form or by any means, electronic, mechanical, photocopying, scanning, recording or otherwise without the prior written permission of the author and the publisher.

Cover design by Paul Mason
Cover illustration by Nigel Pennick

Illustration credits:
Original artwork or photograph by Nigel Pennick: 1. 5, 6, 9, 11, 13, 14, 15, 17, 20, 21, 22, 25, 29, 32, 33, 36, 37, 39, 41, 46, 49, 50, 54, 60, 61, 63, 67, 69, 70.
Nideck Picture Collection: 2, 3, 4, 7, 8, 12, 16, 19, 23, 24, 26, 27, 28, 30, 31, 34, 40, 42, 43, 44, 45, 47, 48, 51, 52, 53, 55, 67, 58, 59, 62, 64, 65, 66, 68.
Rupert Pennick: 35, 38.
Greater London Council: 10, 56.

Published by:

Capall Bann Publishing
Freshfields
Chieveley
Berks
RG20 8TF

Contents

Introduction	1
Chapter 1 Coastal Cataclysms	7
Chapter 2	18
Chapter 3 Flood Legends	33
Chapter 4 Atlantis and Other Sunken Civilisations	42
Cantref y Gwaelod	68
Caer Arianrhod	77
Tyno Helig	78
Scotland	95
North East England	98
Lost Lincolnshire and East Anglia	119
Cromer and Sheringham	122
Eccles	125
Pakefield	128
Dunwich	137
The Dagenham Breach	154
Reculver	156
Goodwin Sands (Lomea)	159
Dover and Folkestone	161
Old Winchelsea	161
Brighthelmstone	168
Selsey	174
Isle of Wight	175
Axmouth	176
A Breton Legend	179
Postscript	186
Bibliography	188

i

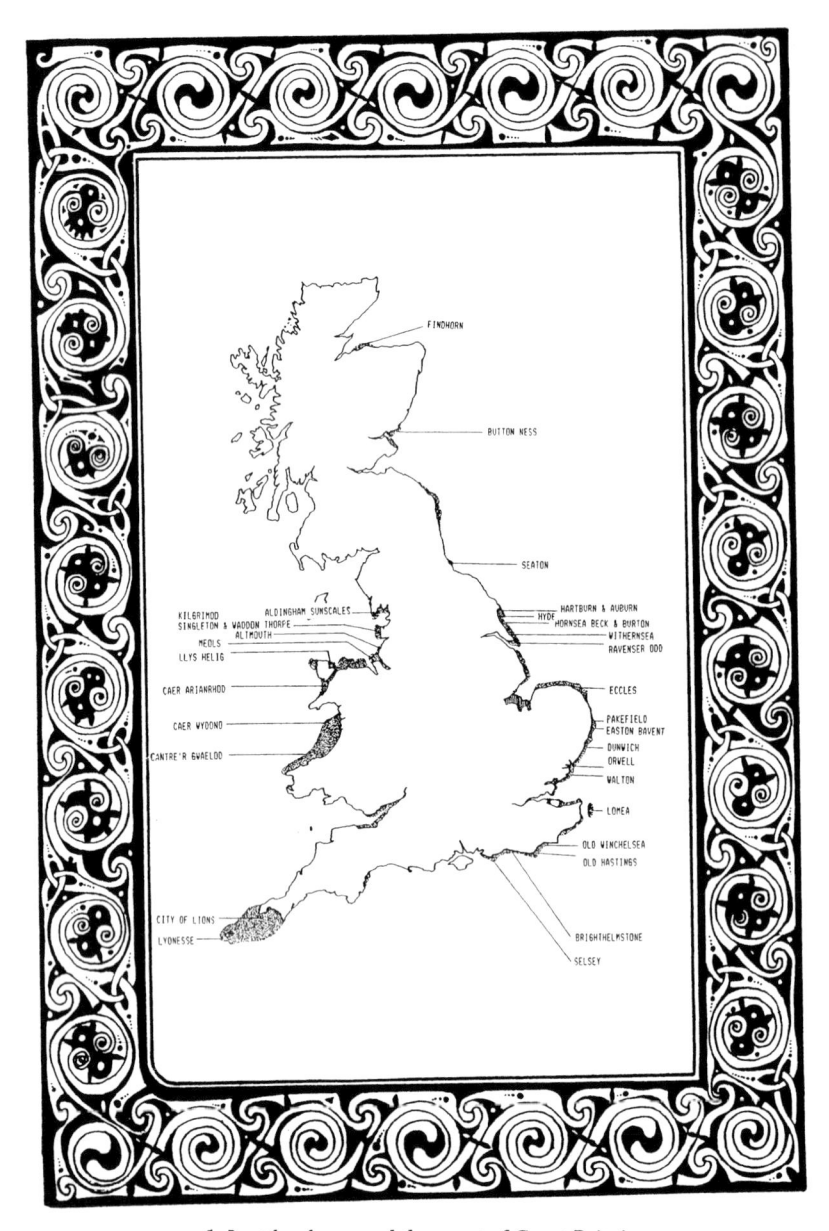

1. Lost lands around the coast of Great Britain.

Introduction

Everyone who has ever studied geography at school knows the familiar outline of the British coast; an outline that appears on modern maps showing topographical, meteorological, administrative and historical information. But although we can be certain that on historical maps, every place-name, road and trackway has been painstakingly checked and re-checked by eminent archaeologists, historians and archivists, the familiar coastal outline is ever-present. Despite the meticulous research behind them, modern historical maps of prehistoric or Roman Britain are invariably inaccurate for they fail to take account of far-reaching changes in the coastline. Apart from the more-or-less legendary lost lands like Lyonesse, which is said to have existed between Cornwall and the Scillies, large tracts of coastal land have vanished from mainland Britain over the last two thousand years.

Whilst some of these territories are remembered only in folklore or legend, others are well documented, having disappeared in the last few centuries. In some places the coastline is now several miles inland of its former position. Flourishing towns have been obliterated, coastal farmland overwhelmed, and forest eradicated.

The singular lack of readily available information on coastal changes has made historians loath to admit their far-reaching significance, yet, without the study of lost legends, many historical documents remain incomprehensible, and the peculiar geographical patterns inland of now-lost territories remain anomalous. This lack of recognition may have been born of ignorance of geophysical processes, of a false assumption that the status quo represents an eternal state, or even from reasons of nationalistic pride; for what patriot would care to admit that Britain, in whose defence he would die rather than yield a square inch of territory, annually lost many acres to the sea? Whatever the reasons for this serious omission, it is a fact that the coastline has altered drastically over the years. The data in this book has been collated from many sources: old chronicles, ancient legends, folktales, Inquisitions and surveys, old maps and hydrographic charts, parish records and county histories. Sometimes fragmentary, sometimes with a wealth of detail, these accounts all testify to the incessant battle of the sea against the land, a battle continuing at this very moment.

Modern scholarship has often found it fashionable to at tempt to discredit the testimony of tradition, yet time and again local lore has been exonerated by archeological excavation. In the case of legendary 'treasures' in burial mounds, this verification has been easy, but with lost lands and vanished towns the gleaning of evidence of that kind is much more difficult. Some times, actual fragments of buildings are found. In June 1981, divers studying the site of the lost city of Dunwich found a stone capital from a medieval building over a quarter of a mile from the present shore. But such finds are rare.

Comparison of old maps with the present day geography is usual!y more fruitful. Many ancient maps, despite the relative unsophistication of ancient instruments, were tolerably accurate, and provide indicators towards areas of study. Ptolemy's map of the British Isles, for instance, whilst considerably inaccurate for the coast of Scotland, tallies reasonably well with the rest of the country, and has the added bonus of possessing a record of latitudes and longitudes for important promontories. From Ptolemy's map we can adduce some interesting observations pertinent to the understanding of coastal changes since 1 50AD. Although the map shows the Isle of Wight, it omits Anglesey, which in Roman times was separated from the mainland only by a fordable creek. Cornwall, too, is shown considerably larger than at present, presumably because Lyonesse was in existence then.

The Merseyside researcher Edward Cox showed the correspondences between Ptolemy's map and the traditional extent of the lost lands bordering the Irish Sea: Morecambe Bay, too, is scarcely shown on Ptolemy's map, which fits in precisely with the known late date of its formation. Many ancient and Renaissance maps show a geography considerably different from that of today. During the last couple of centuries, this variance has been viewed as fanciful invention or just plain inaccuracy, yet several modern archaeological cartographers have pointed out the uncanny correspondences between these ancient maps and the Earth's geography thousands of years ago.

The maps of Ptolemy, Piri Re'is, Andreas Benincasa, Oroniaus Finaeus and Haji Ahmed have all been shown to contain features lost to knowledge in their day but re-discovered during the twentieth century. The Zeno brothers' Map, dating, it is said, from an exploratory voyage undertaken by the Venetians in 1380, shows much of the coastline of northern Europe including Iceland and Greenland. In the seas around Iceland, the Zeno brothers depict several islands that today are no more than sandbanks known for their fishing potential. According to the map, some of these islands were inhabited with towns and cities.

Perhaps we have here the last relics of more ancient maps from which were copied the sites of Thule, Numinor and Hy-Brasil, now lost beneath the waves and relegated to the realm of myth. In addition to maps, there are written sources. For example, it is recorded that as late as the fourth century, the Scillies, now an archipelago of many islets, was but a single large island. In the year 387, a heretic was banished there by the would-be Emperor Maximus.

Geomantic and geographical evidence is found in the patterns formed by seaside roads that now lead nowhere but to the cliff or beach, which, formerly, were access to towns. The unusual distribution of megalithic chambered tombs in Wales and Lancashire also points to the existence of lands now engulfed by the ocean. Relics of lost lands may still be found today in the intertidal zone at low tide. The remains of forests, universally termed 'submarine forests' have been reported on the coasts of Wales, Lancashire, Holderness, Lincolnshire, Norfolk, Kent and

Sussex. The anchorage of Selsey Bill in Sussex, known as the Park, was formerly real parkland, full of game, presided over by a great Saxon cathedral that has long since sunk beneath the waves. The notorious Goodwin Sands, graveyard of many a ship, formerly farmland, was overwhelmed in a great flood. All around the coasts were towns which once flourished and lived the colourful lives of ports, trading centres and fishing communities. Some perished rapidly, engulfed by the raging elements, whilst others fought a protracted rearguard action against the inexorable onward march of the waves, until the last building was grudgingly

With all the lost villages, towns and cities documented here, it is not surprising that a whole mythology and folklore of lost lands has been built up. Despite sometimes fanciful details, the legends almost certainly record actual events. For example, several tell of a man riding on horseback in front of a rapidly advancing tidal wave overwhelming his homeland. Such a tale may appear to be an embellishment until one finds that comparable details were recorded about the 1953 and 1978 East Anglian flood disasters. Unless they had occurred in modern times and had been documented, they would have been dis missed as myth; like those towns whose sole relics are their names, handed down from antiquity to the present day.

Even though the construction of scientifically-designed sea walls over the last hundred years or so has diminished the incidence of coastal destruction, there is still much evidence of erosion. Villages stand on cliff-tops, pale fragments of their former selves. Roads lead nowhere but over the edges of cliffs. Parishes, without churches, are reduced to a handful of fields, and cliff-falls periodically inform us that parts of these islands are still disappearing into the sea. During the nineteenth century, it was estimated that the sea around the coast of Britain washed away land equivalent in area to that of the old county of London. Worldwide, the estimate is twelve square miles a year. In an era when coastal defences were less perfect, even absent, it is ap parent that a not inconsiderable area of our coastline has been claimed by the sea, and with it a large number of towns and villages, each with their own peculiar history and character. Perhaps in the distant future, some British coastal cities, whose names are familiar in every household, might also be remembered only as 'lost cities', engulfed in some cataclysm yet to come.

There is a wealth of lore and recorded history concerning lost Britain, but space precludes comprehensive details of every known event and anecdote. In the following pages, however, beginning at Chapter Six, we explore the major areas of coastal losses, with their associated legends and histories, and attempt to mention most of the known lost towns and villages that once graced these inconstant shores.

2. E. R. Matthews's map of coastal erosion in southern and eastern England.

Chapter 1

Coastal Cataclysms

There are five kinds of event which can lead to the destruction of the land by the sea, causing a real or apparent lowering in land levels sufficient to effect a submergence. Firstly, there are the vast tectonic movements arising from events deep within the earth; displacements on a geologically large scale which have raised mountains or depressed whole continents. Sometimes, these movements have been gradual and almost imperceptible over a grand time scale, but more often they have taken place as sudden cataclysmic displacements. To such rapid actions may be attributed the sudden change that broke the continuity between the early and later Stone Ages.

The second cause is local subsidence unconnected with major tectonic upheavals, due in the main to the collapse of unstable substrata, the leaching out of subterraneous salt beds, slipping of strata over clays, or from the sudden release of underground seas. Recently, the collapse of abandoned mine workings, the extraction of oil and the construction of underground tunnels have been added to the major causes of subsidence.

Thirdly, though less spectacular in scale, is the gradual erosion and denudation caused by the incessant activities of wind and water, which continually wear down exposed lands, gradually altering the landscape piecemeal.

Fourthly, and most importantly in the consideration of lost coastal territories, is the incessant eroding force of tides and storms, undermining cliffs and carrying away movable spoil. Finally, we have the effect of mighty catastrophe in the form of the tsunami or tidal waves, which may be the result of sub marine earthquakes or less commonly by meteor strikes from space. The combined effects of these factors has, over the years, effected drastic changes in British coastal geography.

During the last Ice Age, Britain was covered by a thick layer of ice, rather like the ice-caps that still cover Greenland and Antarctica. Vast quantities of water were tied up here in the form of ice, with the effect that the mean sea level was lowered. The massive weight of ice depressed the land mass, which, during this period, sank deeper into the underlying liquid mantle of the earth. When the climate altered again, melting the ice, the sea level rose dramatically. So did the land, compensating for the sudden loss of its icy burden.

The final consequence of this buoyant uplift of the land, suddenly free from the crushing weight of superincumbent ice, has been the gradual sinking back again into the mantle, like a cork bobbing in the water before finding its equilibrium. Unlike the rapid 'bobbing' of the cork, the time scale involved in land movements is measured in thousands of years. This final settling of the land, combined with the rise in sea level meant that at some time in the relatively recent geological past - the precise date is still not determined with any accuracy - Britain was cut off from continental Europe by this process. At the end of the last Ice Age, the sea level was approximately 400 feet below the present level. Ireland and Britain were then integral with the European continent. Sea levels have risen steadily since then.

But according to data in *The Subsidence of London* published in 1932, borings taken in the lower part of the Thames Valley show that the land surfaces in late neolithic times, about 2000 BC (the era of Stonehenge), now lie between 60 and 70 feet below mean sea level. Even Roman remains under London lie about six feet below the Trinity high water mark.

These discoveries mean that the whole geography of Britain was considerably different in ancient times when the great megalithic monuments like Avebury. Stonehenge, Callanish and Stanton Drew were erected. Any theories concerning the movement of

3. Columns of the Temple of Serapis at Pozzuoli, Italy.

Seventeenth-century map purporting to show the form of Atlantis in the Atlantic Ocean between the Old and New Worlds.

stones from Mynydd Preseli in Wales to Salisbury Plain for Stonehenge must take into account the quite different topography.

Elsewhere in Europe, ancient geography was also different from today s familiar outlines. Part of Syracuse in Sicily, Leptis Magna in Libya, the port of Corinth, Cenchrae in Greece, and the ancient harbours of Caesarea and Baiae have all sunk beneath the Mediterranean; a sea which has no appreciable tides. In the Mediterranean, all lost towns must have been submerged by the action of earthquakes or tectonic subsidence. Evidence is widespread.

One prime example is the famous Temple of Serapis at Pozzuoli, in Italy, which some time after its construction in the Classical period sank into the sea to about one third the height of its columns. These were then attacked by marine organisms which bored holes into the marble. Finally, the land rose, and by the end of the eighteenth century the temple was again clear of the waves in the Bay of Baiae.

The Mediterranean is, of course, famed for its volcanic activity. The volcanoes of Stromboli, Vesuvius and Etna still erupt occasionally, and the archetypal island of Vulcano, named after the Roman God of fire, still rises 1500 feet out of the Mediterranean. Earthquakes are unfortunately commonplace along the shores of the Mediterranean, and the site of one of the greatest volcanic cataclysms known can still be visited on the island of Santorini. There, in about 1500 BC, the island was literally blown apart by an eruption of gargantuan proportions. One school of Atlantologists believes the eruption to be the origin of legends about Atlantis.

Whatever the origin of the Atlantis legend may be, it is certain that large tracts of Mediterranean coastal regions have been lost; for many written accounts still exist to tell of these catastrophes. The Peloponnesian Wars, by the Greek author Thucydides (460-400BC), tells us: *"The sea at Orobiai in Euboia... rising in a great wave, covering a part of the city; and then subsided in some places, but in others the flooding was permanent, and what was formerly land is now sea. The people who could not escape to high ground perished."*

In the time of Virgil, there was a tradition that Sicily had formerly been connected to the Italian mainland. This is alluded to in *The Aenid*. Dryden's translation of Virgil's masterwork gives it thus:

> *"...Th' Italian shore*
> *And fair Sicilian coast were one before .*
> *An earthquake caused the flaw: the roaring tides,*
> *The passage broke, that land from land divides,*
> *And where the lands retired, the rushing ocean rides."*
> (iii, 414)

Philo Judaeus (BC 20 - AD 40) also commented on the severance of Sicily: *"Consider how many districts on the mainland, not only such as were near the coast, but even such as were completely inland, have been swallowed up by the waters: and consider how great a proportion of land has become sea and is now sailed over by innumerable ships. Who is ignorant of that most sacred Sicilian strait, which in old times joined Sicily to the continent of Italy?"* Philo also refers to three Greek cities that were submerged: Aigara, Boura and Helike.

Helike sank beneath the Gulf of Corinth in an earthquake. For centuries afterwards, it was visible from boats, and provided a tourist attraction to wealthy Roman visitors. Boatmen made a good living ferrying the sightseers over the ruins and pointing out the important civic buildings and the statue of Zeus which remained standing though submerged.

In the Aegean, the ruins of another submerged city have been seen near Melos, and along the Adriatic coast of Croatia, where the continuation of Roman land-survey patterns onto offshore islands attest to their former connection with the mainland. Many ancient remains of Classical civilisation still exist at the bottom of the Mediterranean. The underwater explorer

Commander Cousteau once recounted that during a dive he came across a paved road far out in the depths of the Mediterranean. He followed it for some distance,

Elsewhere in the world, similar ruins abound. Although some underwater fragments - like the famous 'Bimini Road', hailed as evidence of the lost Atlantis - may be enigmatic natural formations, many known 'lost' towns have been found. In Azerbaijan, a submerged town exists in the Bay of Baku, and blocks of stone bearing inscriptions and carvings have been fished up from time to time. Off Mahabalipuram, Madras, India, there are the remains of a sunken city, and in the Gulf of Mexico, near Cozumel, archaeologists have studied submerged buildings of the Mayan civilisation. In 1966, reports were published of a Dr Menzie's discovery of submerged ruins Iying at the astonishing depth of 6,000 feet beneath the waves of the Pacific Ocean, off the coast of Peru. This last-mentioned claim was immediately hailed by lost lands aficionados as the rediscovery of the continent of Mu.

Earthquakes are not usually associated with Britain in the popular mind, yet the catalogue of British earth upheavals is long and ancient. Ancient chronicles, especially those preserved in the English cathedrals, attest to many severe earthquakes, some of which caused great loss of life and material destruction. Many records are also preserved in a curious compilation, published in 1749 by Dr Thomas Short, F.R.S. Titled *A General Chronological History of the Air, Meteors, Weather, Seasons, Meteors, etc.*, the treatise, compiled during sixteen years of research, lists many strange and extreme events. *"These scraps of history", wrote Short, "lay scattered in a vast multitude of authors of different designs and professions..."* until the learned doctor collected and catalogued them. Short, who, unfortunately, rarely gives his authorities, records several earthquakes that may have affected the British coastline. Among them are the great earthquakes of Wales in AD 394, which *"made sad havoc"*, and the Cornish earthquake of AD 424, where there were *"great losses, many killed"*. These, and other now unverifiable records, may account for the loss of Cantref y Gwaelod. the 'Lost Lowland

Hundred' of Wales, and the celebrated land of Lyonesse; if a major subsidence of land accompanied the quakes.

Floods and coastal losses have been occasioned by more recent British earthquakes. On April 6th 1580, at six o'clock in the evening, a great earthquake struck southern England; the shocks being felt as far away as France, and the Low Countries. Part of the cliff and castle wall at Dover were thrown down into the English Channel by the seismic shock. In 1692, an earthquake at Framlingham in Suffolk caused the flooding of the town. In the same year, Jamaica suffered a catastrophic earthquake in which a tract of land near to the town of Port Royal, over 1,000 acres in extent, sank in less than a minute beneath the waves of the Caribbean.

During the English 'Great Earthquake' of April 22nd, 1884, a member of Parliament was standing on the balcony of the Palace of Westminster looking at the Thames. At the moment of the seismic shock, the MP made his way to the balustrade and noted *"a wave about three foot high sweep across the river and swamp several small boats"*. This seismically generated wave is a common consequence of earthquakes near or below the sea.

T he speed with which these walls of water can move depends on the depth of the water through which they are travelling. but can be as much as 450 miles per hour. The fsunarrli. as the Japanese call it. is always preceded by an abnormal withdrawal of the sea from its usual level, followed, sometimes after several hours, by a loud noise as the water returns in the form of an enormous wave advancing at a great rate.

The effects of tsunamis are devastating. After the volcanic eruption of Thera in AD 365, a tsunami in the eastern Mediterranean threw a ship two miles inland on the Peloponnesian coast and carried the ships moored in Alexandria harbour over the houses and into the surrounding countryside. When the great Indonesian marine volcano Krakatoa erupted in 1883, waves up to 100 feet high broke, with devastating force over all the neighbouring coasts, killing more than 50.000 people. Even large stone buildings are no match for tsunamis of this magnitude. In 1946, an undersea earthquake in the Aleutian Islands produced a tidal wave that swept away a sturdy stone lighthouse which stood 100 feet above sea level on the Alaskan coast. A tsunami which hit Japan in May 1960 was only 30 feet high, small by Krakatoan standards, nevertheless it swept away 5,000 houses and wrecked 33,000 others.

Although the Santorini eruption of circa 1500 BC and that of Krakatoa in 1883 produced the largest tsunamis on record, they are not restricted to the Pacific or the Mediterranean. There is ample evidence of tidal wave activity around the shores of northern Europe. The great Lisbon earthquake of November Ist, 1775, caused a tsunami 50 feet high which devastated the coasts of Spain, Portugal, the Azores and northwest Africa. The worst earthquake to hit Iberia, since antiquity, wiped out over 60,000 people, and did terrible damage around the coastline. "*Some 3,000 people who had taken refuge on a new stone quay, or jetty,*" wrote D. Morgan Thomas in *The Day Book of Wonders*, "*were submerged by a vast mountain wave. It came rolling in from the sea upon the land, sweeping all before it, and in an instant turned over the whole quay and every person on it, with all the vessels moored to it, so that not a vestige of them ever appeared again. Where that quay stood, was afterwards found a depth of 600 feet of water.*" The Lisbon tsunami was felt as far away as the Pomeranian coast of Poland, where ships were flung onto the land. Tsunamis were fairly common at one time in the Baltic, going under the name 'sea bears', and the traditions of Brittany, Cornwall and Wales tell of towns inundated in the same manner of the Lisbon jetty.

If, at some time during the first millennium of the Christian Era, the western coasts of Britain were overtaken by a tsunami, then the devastation wrought would have rendered those areas uninhabitable. Vulnerable towns would have been obliterated, and, although some lands might not have been immediately submerged, any existing coastal defences would have been broken down, allowing the normal processes of erosion to begin. If our tsunami was the result of an earthquake, then it is

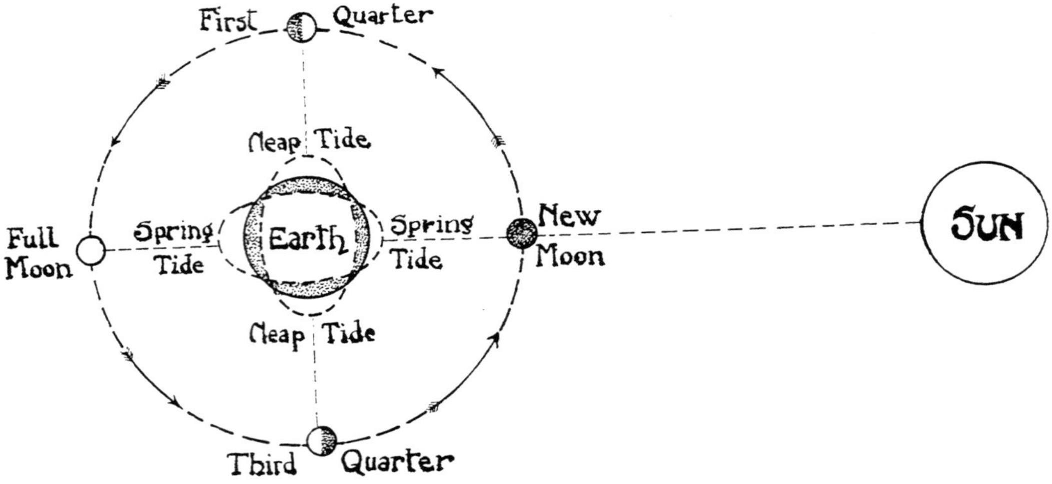

5. How the interaction of the positions of the Moon and the Sun causes the tides in the oceans on Earth.

possible there was a sudden fall in the land level. Geological evidence at Barry in south Wales, and at Chepstow, points to a subsidence of between 42 and 55 feet. The recurrent folk-tale of a sudden wave wiping out all in its path has a ring of truth, and such an important event would have become indelibly impressed upon oral tradition, like those that remain to this day.

In a society in which religious belief was a matter of everyday life, such a cataclysm would certainly have been seen in terms of divine retribution, and, indeed, we find in the legends a moralistic tone that those who perished in the floods were sinners who deserved their fate. In our age of unbelief, we like to think they were just unlucky.

Chapter 2

> When I have seen by Time s fell hand defaced
> The rich proud cost of outworn buried age;
> When sometimes lofty towers I see down-razed
> And brass eternal slave to mortal rage:
> When I have seen the hungry ocean gain
> Advantage from the kingdom of the shore
> And the firm soil win of the watery main.
> Increasing store with loss and loss with store...
> Shakespeare, Sonnet 64.

Many towns along the east coast of England bear the scars of severe and repeated flooding. Even when parts of them have not permanently succumbed to coastal inundation, much damage has been sustained. In some towns the observant visitor may see a salty line several feet or even yards high upon walls of old and not-so-old buildings, and a conversation with a local inhabitant will elicit reminiscences of the great flood of 1953, or whenever the last major inroad of the sea occurred.

Other places display painted signs, brass plaques, inset stones or lines incised on walls recording the height to which the floodwaters rose on some notable night. King's Lynn in Norfolk has several embedded in the wall of a church recording the floods of 1883,]949, 1953, 1961 and 1978; whilst at Blakeney cast metal plates bolted to a wall show the levels reached on 'Black Monday' 1897 and during the disastrous 1953 inundation.

These drastic effects have been largely the result of several gales occurring in conjunction with high tides. Tides rise and fall twice in just over 24 hours, caused by a complex interaction between the gravitational fields of the Earth, the Moon and the Sun. The Moon has the most influence. This fundamental connection between the phases of the Moon and the tides, had a profound effect upon early humanity, whose interest in astronomy no doubt arose from the wish to predict the highs and lows of the tidal cycle.

These highs and lows, the Spring and Neap Tides are very important, for at Spring Tide the possibility of flooding occurs. Later, the necessity of navigation itself bound up with the tides, led to the development of complex astronomy. Perhaps the erection of megalithic stone circles as lunar computers stems from a desire to predict the tidal cycle. Tidal range gradually alters in conjunction with the phases of the Moon. The Spring Tides (the word Spring comes from an old Norse word meaning swelling) take place every two weeks just after the full and new moons. Neap Tides come every other week, having the least difference between high and low water levels.

Spring Tides are dangerous when they occur in conjunction with bad weather. Then a stormy surge may occur. This is a situation where the sea is whipped up to a great height by the combined action of the tide and the wind. The wind causes the surface of the sea to slope. If this continues for long enough, the slope becomes stationary by getting into balance with the force of the continuously-blowing wind. For the North Sea a wind blowing from the north-west is the most dangerous; for a wind blowing the full length of the North Sea and causing a gradient of 1 in 300,000 (ie. 1 inch in 4.7 miles), stretching the full 570 miles from Scotland to the Dutch coast will produce a 10 foot surge over and above normal high tide level. The worst east coast floods from 1287 to 1978 have occurred in this way.

People living in coastal areas have always lived in fear of such storm surges. Writing in December 1287, John Oxnead described such a flood caused by the sea breaching the Horsey Gap in Norfolk. *"The sea in dense darkness began to be agitated by the violence of the wind and burst through its accustomed limits, overwhelming towns, fields, and inundating parts which no age in past times had recorded to be covered with water. For, issuing forth about the middle of the night, it suffocated or drowned men and women sleeping in their beds, with infants in their cradles,*

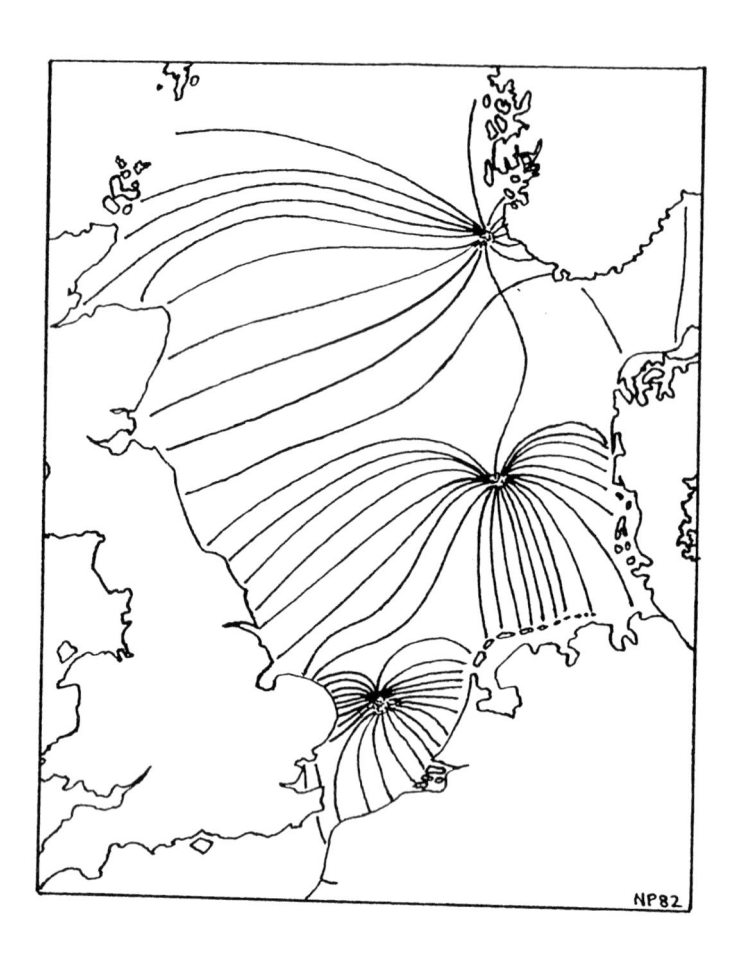

6. Co-tidal lines. On average, high water occurs at the same time at all points on any line, in chronological order.

and many types of livestock. Many, surrounded by the waters, sought refuge by climbing trees, but, benumbed by the cold, they fell into the water and were drowned."

Frisia and Schleswig-Holstein, on the south-eastern boundaries of the North Sea, retain a continuous record of such storm-surges. In his 1666 *Nordfresische Chronika*, Heimreich records that in the year 1030 Heiligland on Sudstrand contained nine parishes, but that after the great floods of 1202 and 1216 "*But two churches remained*". These two finally disappeared in the great deluge of 1362. Neocorus, the '*Dithmarsch Chronicler*' (circa 1590), asserted that in the 1362 disaster, "*between flood and ebb tide, 200,000 folk were drowned.*" The Eiderstedt Chronicle tells us that in the "*Year 1362 at midnight there came the greatest of floods, then were drowned most of the folk of Utland.*"

Massive floods taking horrendous toll were unfortunately not uncommon in former times. The 'St Elizabeth Flood' of 1421 engulfed 72 villages in the Netherlands, killing an estimated 10,000. On October 5th, 1570, a storm surge hit the east coast of England causing incalculable damage. Between Grimsby and Humberston buildings were washed away and 20,000 head of livestock drowned. The sea broke through between Wisbech and Walsoken and flooded the countryside for ten miles around, and at Harwich a new sea wall was utterly destroyed.

In 1607, another storm surge caused massive damage in East Anglia. Reclaimed marshland was flooded and the sea wall between Happisburgh and Great Yarmouth was washed away. In 1613 the Fens were again inundated. At Terrington the sea defences crumbled before the raging waves, and over 2,000 head of livestock perished. Wisbech was again flooded, and as in the 1570 flood, the Walsoken sea wall was swept away. 1703 saw the celebrated 'Great Gale' immortalised by Daniel Defoe. This caused such an enormous loss of life and shipping, that Queen Anne ordered a day of fasting, penitence and prayer that there should never again be such a storm. On February 16th, 1736, just such a storm recurred. A tidal surge flooded the coastline

7. A contemporary engraving of the extensive floods of 1607.

22

from Kent to Lincolnshire. Sea walls were beaten down, and many perished in the ensuing floods. That February, a correspondent to *The Gentleman's Magazine* wrote: "*The little isles of Canvey and Foulness were quite under water, not a hoof was saved, and the inhabitants were taken away from the upper part of their houses into boats.*"

Bad floods continued through the nineteenth century. In March, 1883, north-west Norfolk suffered further. A tidal wave surged through the streets of King's Lynn, and many were seized with panic. At Hunstanton, the sea water raced along the Front, carrying away everything that was not a fixture. November 29th, 1897 was long known in East Anglia as Black Monday, for on that day northerly gales, coinciding with a Spring Tide, caused the by-now familiar pattern of devastation, flooding almost the entire length of the coast from north Norfolk to the Essex part of the Thames estuary. The tide hit the coast at mid-day, so there were no human fatalities.

By far the worst coastal inundation of modern times in Britain was the great flood of Saturday January 31st, 1953, when the coasts of these isles were subjected to severe storms combined with a surge tide. In the Irish Sea, the British Railways car ferry Princess Victoria was sunk by the hurricane-force winds with the loss of 132 passengers. This ghastly toll was made ironically worse as it included all of the women and children aboard, who perished when their specially-reserved lifeboat capsized in the winter seas as it was being launched.

Thousands of acres of Scottish forest were flattened by the winds, but it was on the east coast that the greatest disaster was in store. The severe north westerly gales piled up the Spring Tide to a level eight feet higher than normal. Naturally, the surge tides, driven by hurricane-like winds, found the sea defences' weakest points, and catastrophe was inevitable. The final toll of the storm was 307 people dead, over 400 houses obliterated, 32,000 forced to flee and thousands of acres of land flooded with sea water.

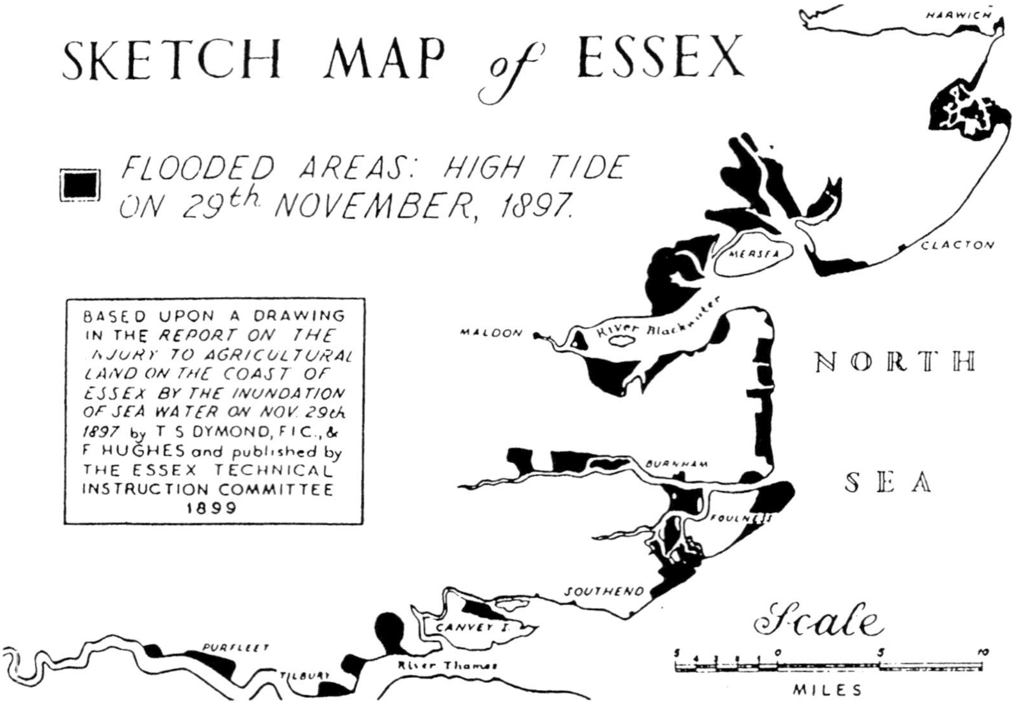

SKETCH MAP of ESSEX

■ FLOODED AREAS: HIGH TIDE ON 29th NOVEMBER, 1897.

BASED UPON A DRAWING IN THE REPORT ON THE 'INJURY TO AGRICULTURAL LAND ON THE COAST OF ESSEX BY THE INUNDATION OF SEA WATER ON NOV. 29th 1897' by T S DYMOND, F.I.C., & F HUGHES and published by THE ESSEX TECHNICAL INSTRUCTION COMMITTEE 1899

The 1953 flood is a long catalogue of disasters. The following incidents are typical of many. At Saltfleet in Lincolnshire, four people were drowned when their bungalows were swept away by a sudden huge wave. At Sutton-on-Sea, 300 years of sand dunes which formerly protected the town from the sea were levelled in a few minutes. The manner of destruction was the same all along the coast: a huge wave would suddenly inundate a town, the water rising several feet in a few seconds, drowning many before they had time to realise what was happening. This wave was invariably caused by the sudden final breaching of sand dunes or the sea wall by the surging tide. Survivors from Lincolnshire to Essex recount hearing a terrific roar, and scrambling upstairs to safety before their houses were flooded to a depth of ten feet or more.

Passengers on the Hunstanton to King's Lynn railway line had a nasty experience that night. A quarter of a mile south of Hunstanton station, the 7:27 pm. train hit water. The crew decided to keep going, as the water was not high enough to extinguish the fire of the steam locomotive. But about one hundred yards further on, a wooden bungalow suddenly came floating across the tracks in front of the train, collided with it and brought the locomotive to an abrupt halt. This was the battered remains of a bungalow park' between Heacham and Hunstanton, where 65 people were drowned; those fortunate enough to be saved lost all their worldly goods. On Canvey Island in Essex, there were 58 deaths and the entire population of 11,500 was made homeless. There, the sea wall had been breached at about midnight, and a massive wave had overwhelmed the whole low-lying island in a few seconds.

On Monday, February 2nd, 1953, Charles Garner flew over the devastation. *'The familiar curve of East Anglia"*, he reported, *"the Estuaries. the Thames Mouth islands, firm enough lines in your school atlases, now have no boundaries but are at the will of the sea"*. The magnitude of the 1953 disaster was such that it took several years before life in affected towns returned to normal; and of course for those who had lost family and home life was never the same again. But in the present modern era, the

25

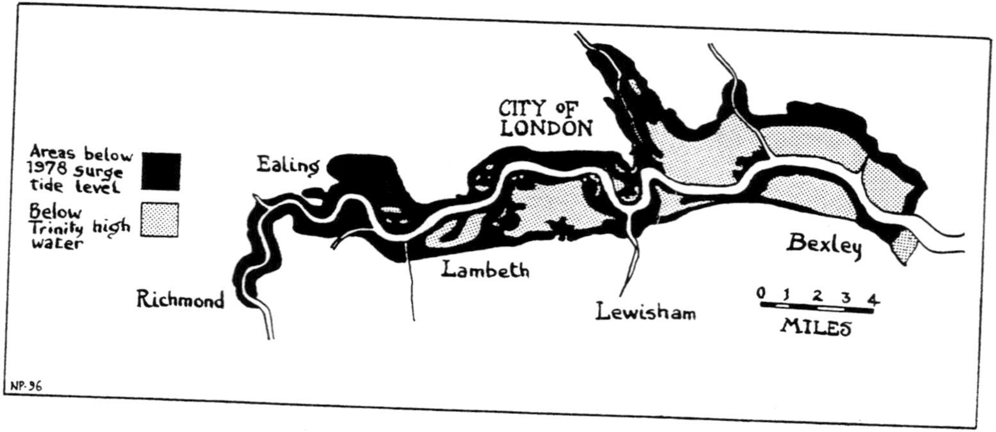

9. *The 1978 surge almost flooded a large tract of land in around London.*

technical knowhow and material backup is such that breached sea walls can be repaired, towns can be rebuilt and life can resume again, almost as before.

Even though the disaster occurred in modern times, with all the resources of an advanced and prosperous country, clear ing up the mess was a difficult enough task, despite mechanised tools and powered vehicles. Mud up to a foot thick covered the mound, drinking water was contaminated, domestic and farm animals perished in their thousands, and at Sea Palling and Sutton-on-Sea, sand filled some houses almost to ceiling level. When a cataclysm of such dimensions occurred in ancient times, there was no back-up which could clear up the ruins, such areas were invariably abandoned. Sea walls breached were hen left unrepaired, and further inroads of the tide continued he work of destruction, leading eventually to the complete victory of the sea, and the permanent loss of the land. All traces of human habitation would soon have been extirpated, and the only indication that inhabited land had existed there would be the lingering legends.

Even in the 1950s, the soil was contaminated by salt water; over 170,000 acres were rendered infertile. In some places, for instance the marshes near Great Yarmouth, it was not possible to graze cattle for two and a half years afterwards. Even the modern sophisticated sea walls erected after the 1953 floods can only be a temporary measure, for the sea's erosive force is ever-present. Today, the concrete sea wall of 1954 at Sea Palling in Norfolk (near the site of the lost town of Eccles), is being undermined, and has recently had extra steel reinforcements added to it. Such rapid attrition inevitably means that another serious breach will occur before long.

At the time of writing, the last serious inroad of the sea along the east coast of England was occasioned by a force 12 gale and surge tide on January 11th 1978. That surge breached the river defences at several places along the south shore of the Humber, causing flooding up to four feet deep. At Cleethorpes, the sea wall was broken down and a thousand houses were flooded. A

10. Advertisement printed in local London newspapers in the 1970s by the now-suppressed Greater London Council warning Londoners of the procedure to be taken in time of flood warning.

headline in *The Grimsby Telegraph* described the storm as "Resort's Worst Disaster". On the pier, 150 people, including children and disabled people in wheelchairs, were enjoying a performance of the pantomime Mother Goose when the sea tore away a 20 foot section of the wooden decking between the theatre and the land. They were rescued by policemen who improvised a 'tightrope of planks'. The same storm ripped the pier at Skegness completely in two, leaving a twisted mass of wreckage.

Further south, in Cambridgeshire, Wisbech was inundated by rapidly-rising floodwaters whilst the centre of King's Lynn was flooded to a depth even greater than that of the 1953 flood. Over 500 houses were swamped in the low-lying areas between Millfleet and Purfleet. "*The centuries-old council chamber had never seen a sight like it,*" reported *The Lynn News and Advertiser*, "*Procedure went by the board as the councillors beat a hasty retreat from the building without waiting for the meeting to be adjourned. Some got wet feet as they ran through water lapping near the front door in Queen Street.*" In both the 1883 and 1978 floods, people seeking refuge were seen running through the streets in advance of the tidal wave. Stories like this, recorded at the time, closely echo the details in the tales of lost lands, usually dismissed as no more than legend. One survivor of the 1953 flood at Saltfleet unknowingly re-enacted the ancient scenario, now preserved as myth: "*The tidal wave stretched as far as I could see and I only survived by running inland as fast as I could go.*"

The 1978 flood also finished off the pier at Hunstanton, leaving only the end of it standing, isolated, out to sea. Along the coast at Wells-next-the-Sea, a stand of large Corsican Pines planted after the 1953 flood was battered down by the waves which breached the Beach Road defences, which themselves had been strengthened after the 1953 disaster. Cruisers and yachts were swept into and deposited in the High Street, whilst high and dry on the quay stood the coaster Function, incongruously juxtaposed with French's Fish Bar. At Walcott, which had seen the sea wall undermined in 1969 and breached in 1976, the sea compounded the damage of two years previously and ripped away a large

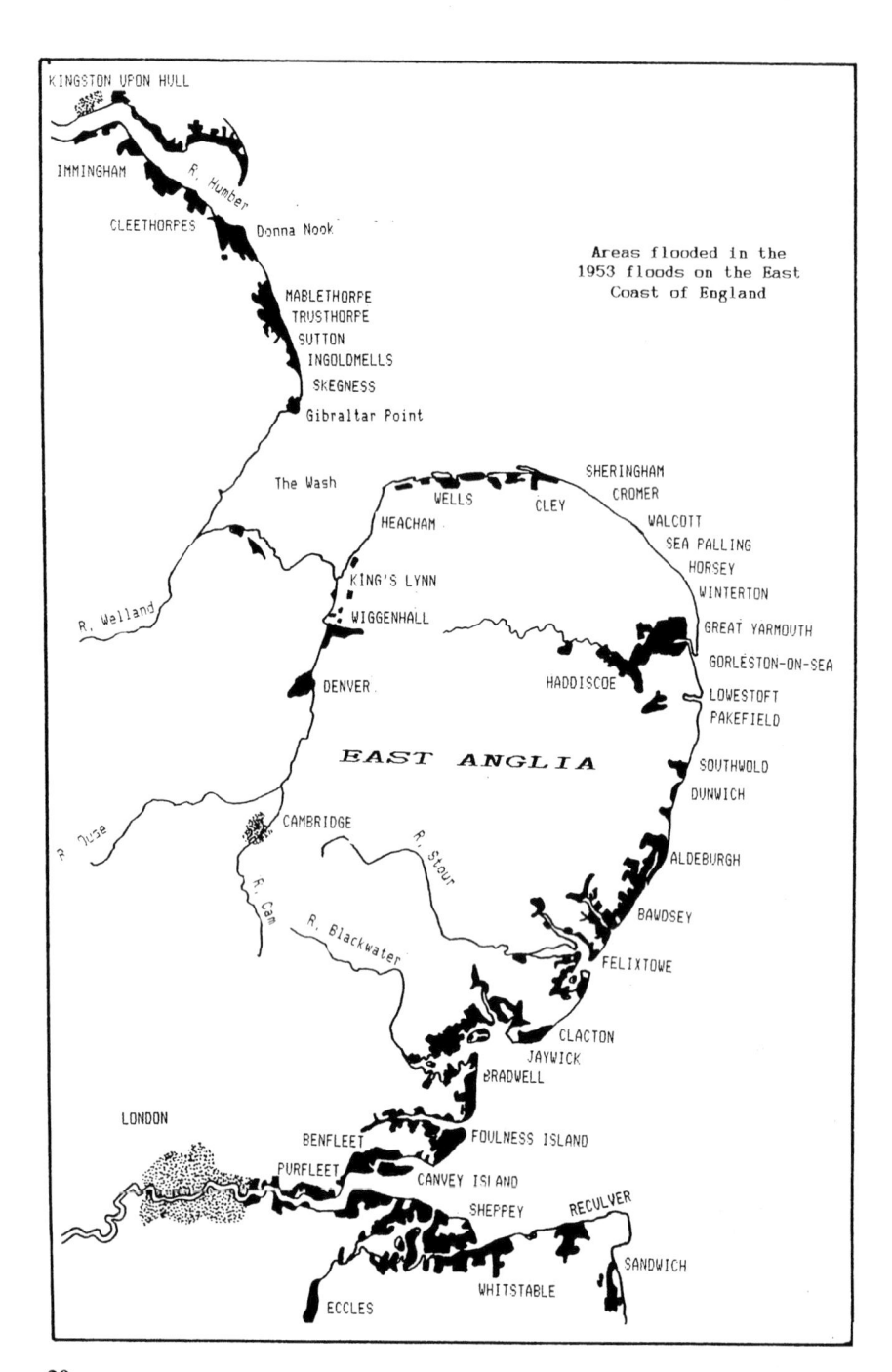

Areas flooded in the 1953 floods on the East Coast of England

section of cliff. Had the tide risen by another twelve inches, then London would have been added to the toll of flooded towns. The storm surge would have overtopped the embankments which keep the metropolis from being sub merged at high tide. Fortunately, the surge abated further south and the flood warning sirens did not sound over the capital.

12. A medieval interpretation of the building of Noah's Ark.

Chapter 3

Flood Legends

"The Moon's chariot will run amok in the Zodiac and the Seven Sisters will burst into tears. . . in the twinkling of an eye the seas shall rise up and the arena of the winds shall be open once again."
                Merlin, *The Prophecies.*

Most cultures with a developed mythology possess legends of a universal flood. Some commentators see this fact as the fulfilment of an archetypal human feeling; others as indicative of historical local floods which their interpreters saw as covering the whole world. Those holding fundamentalist religious beliefs assert that these legends are all affirmations of the celebrated Noachian Flood of the Bible. It is probable that there are several origins, because flood myths exist in almost every culture.

The story of Noah and his Ark is too well known to be recounted here in detail. In Irish mythology, a man named Brith, his wife Birren and their son and daughter Lara and Cessair escaped the universal flood in a boat which finally came ashore in Inisfail (Ireland). One version of the tale places the flood's origin in a magic barrel, which, when opened by a curious woman, gave out a never- ending stream of water that over flowed the entire world.

The ancient Greek flood story parallels the Jewish Biblical myth. Zeus, tired of the profligate and violent ways of mankind, decided to wipe out humanity and create anew. After toying with the idea of incinerating the Earth, he decided that drowning was a better fate for the degenerates. However, not all were to perish, for he would save but two people - Deucalion, son of Prometheus, and his wife Pyrrha, daughter of Pandora. In order that they might be saved, Zeus instructed Deucalion to construct a large wooden chest and for the couple to get into it. The flood occurred when "*All of a sudden enormous volumes of water issued from the Earth*", relates Lucian in his De Deae Syriae, written in 170 BC, "*and rains of extraordinary abundance began to fall; the rivers left their beds, and the sea overflowed its shores; the whole Earth was covered with water and all men perished.*"

When Zeus unleashed his purifying deluge upon the world, the couple, floating in their chest, were spared. After nine days, the chest came to rest upon a mountain in Thessaly, and the couple waited there for the waters to subside. Hermes was despatched thence as Zeus' messenger to see what the survivors wanted. Deucalion answered that they needed companions, so they were ordered to pick up the rocks on the holy mountain upon which they had landed. These rocks, the bones of Mother Earth, were then thrown over the survivors' shoulders. Wherever they landed, they were magically transformed into human beings: women from those thrown by Pyrrha and men from Deucalion. The Sumerian flood-myth naturally parallels the Jewish version - one may have given rise to the other. The Assembly of Gods decided to eliminate mankind by flood. One benevolent god, Enki, resolved to help the humans, and warned Zuisudra, the King of Shurrupak, to build an ark. Only Ziusudra survived the ensuing deluge, and was rewarded by the gift of immortality.

A similar tale was told in ancient Babylonia. There, the god Enlil so hated the human race that he persuaded Anu to cause a flood to destroy it. However, the god Ea warned Utnapishtim to make a boat and take aboard all sorts of animals to continue life after the floods had subsided. After seven days of continuous tempest, the rain ceased, and the boat came aground on Mount Nisir. Utnapishtim opened the hatch and dispatched a dove, which returned, then a swallow, which also returned. Finally, he sent out a raven which did not come back. Then Utnapishtim opened all the hatches and released all the creatures onto the mountain. Then he performed a sacrifice of thanksgiving for his delivery. Enlil, enraged that someone had survived his deluge, resolved to exterminate the hapless survivors, but the other gods bade him spare them, saying that the righteous did not deserve to perish with the wicked. Enlil relented, and bestowed immortality on Utnapishtim and his spouse. The likeness of this legend to the Biblical version is very strong, only the gods' names and the birds released have been altered.

In Hebrew mythology, the mountain upon which Noah's Ark alighted was Ararat, otherwise known as Koh-i-Noor, often translated as 'The Mountain of Light', a name also given to the sacred jewel of the Sikh faith which is now incorporated in the British Crown Jewels. One of the holy mountains of the Mazdean faith, Ararat is occasionally in the news when explorers report the sighting of fragments reputed to be the remains of Noah's Ark somewhere in a glacier. However, a real ark is unlikely, as Mount Ararat is not the only mountain with a claim to hold relics of the Noachian Ark. In his *History of Syria*, Nicholas Damascenus states that in his time (circa 40 BC), the remains of the Ark existed on Mount Baris. Perhaps devotees of the ancient Ark cults constructed replica arks on their favourite holy mountains!

Ancient Indian mythology has no fewer than five versions of the flood legend, one in the Rig Veda and four in the Upangas. In these tales, a magic fish warns Manu, son of Vivasvat of the impending deluge: *"The period dreadful for the Universe moving and fixed has come. Make for thyself a strong ship, with a cable attached; embark in it with the seven Rishis and stow in it, carefully preserved and assorted all the seeds which have been anciently described by the Brahmans."* Manu did as he was told, and survived. His ship, towed by the supernatural fish, finally came to rest on the highest peak of Himavat, a mountain named ever since Naubandhana, the 'Binding of the Ship'.

This Indian deluge was seen as a *'dissolution of the Universe'*, a cataclysm that marks the dividing-point between distinct world ages. During these eras of purification, the whole is submerged in the ocean. This idea also existed in Norse mythology. The great German scholar Willibrord Kirfel showed in his magnificent work *Die Cosmographie der Inder*, published in 1920, that the duration of these cycles were mathematically related to cosmic concepts. The numbers associated in Norse myths with the construction of Valhalla are intimately tied up with Indian cosmography. In the Indian tradition, Kali Yuga, the last and most dissolute age of mankind, contains 432,000 years. In Norse tradition, the great hall of the Slain, Valhalla, possesses 540 gates through each of which 800 Einherjar, the 'chosen ones' of Odin's bodyguard, ride out to do battle on Ragnarok, the Last Day.

The echoes of ancient Indo-European cosmology are unmistakable, for Kali Yuga, too, ends in cosmic cataclysm. The Mazdean version of the flood story can be found in the Iranian holy book The Zend-Avesta. Here, Yima is warned by the supreme deity of light, Ahura Mazda, of the impending cataclysm. The god orders Yima to build a vessel in which seeds, animals and the essences of nature are enclosed. This vessel alone is spared destruction by the waters, and Yima is advised of the flood's end by a bird, Karshipta, messenger of the god. This old Persian account of the deluge attributes the flood to a fiery dragon from the south, which can be interpreted as volcanic activity.

In Norse mythology, too, the extermination of the land by Surt, the Fire Giant, is the prelude to the universal deluge at Ragnarok. It was not without reason that the new volcanic island which rose from the Atlantic Ocean near Iceland in the early 1960's was dubbed Surtsey or Surt's Island.

Central American mythology names the survivor of the world inundation as Coxcox, otherwise called Teocipactli or Tezpi. Along with his wife Xochiquetzal, Coxcox was saved in a boat made from cypress-wood, the wood of Noah's Ark. The pair set sail along with their children, animals and seeds whose survival was essential to the continuance of human life on earth. After a period aimlessly drifting on the ocean, Coxcox sent forth a vulture, but it did not return. Other birds were despatched, but finally a humming-bird returned to the ship bearing a leafy branch in its bill. The intrepid mariner then grounded his ship on the mountain of Colhuacan, whose element huaca attests to its holiness.

The tradition of this New World Noah has been found among the Aztec, Mixtec, Tlascalan and Zapotec nations of ancient central America. Among the Maya, a similar flood legend is recounted in their holy book the Popol Vuh, and to the north, storytellers of the native tribes still recount their own versions of the tale. The Chippewa tribe had a deluge survivor called Menaboshu, the Delawares' was Nanabush, whilst the hero of the Mandans' flood was called Numohkmuchanah. Similar stories have been gathered from the Iroquois, the Chickasaws, the Sioux and the Okanaguas.

Ignatius Donnelly, author of the monumental work *Atlantis: the Antediluvian World*, categorised the common features of deluge legends worldwide: The founder of the race or nation is warned of the coming disaster, but others disregard the warning. There is a vast conflagration - caused by a comet, the Moon or some other extraterrestrial visitor - but this is extinguished by a flood. The founder escapes with his family and livestock, either on a ship, or by climbing a high mountain. If on board ship, he sends out birds to check whether the flood has subsided. Eventually, he reaches dry land, usually a mountain, where he finds other survivors.

In Britain, we have the Welsh flood legend where the two brothers Dwyfan and Dwyfach escape by boat. Trevilian, the survivor of Lyonesse, and Gradlon, the king of Ker Ys, both escaped to higher ground on horseback. Both Gradlon and Helig ap Glannawg were warned, before the overwhelming of their lands, that retribution for their sins is imminent. Trevilian founded the famous Cornish family that still flourishes today, whilst the sons of the Welsh flood survivors became Christian holy men and did good works.

These legends are in the mainstream of universal deluge myths. The flood-myth of Nordic Europe takes a somewhat different form from the conventional tale, for it is told as a future event which is destined to occur at Ragnarok, the Last Day. Then, according to Norse belief, the gods will be overthrown in a final battle with the demonic empire. After the gods and demons have all eliminated each other, Surt, the fire giant, will throw flame and lal fire over the whole earth, after which it will sink beneath the waves th of a universal deluge. After this apocalypse, the All-Father, the supreme deity beyond and above the gods of Asgard, will cause a new earth to rise from beneath the waves. They will come forth to re-populate the new earth in an era freed from evil and suffering.

Some interpreters of Ragnarok have seen in the curious tale echoes of a cosmic disaster in antiquity, handed down in folk-memory over millennia and finally formalised into a myth about the future. The ancients, with their belief in the cyclic nature of history, would have seen accounts of an ancient cataclysm that ended a former era as presaging a future disaster that would end the present one. The tale is preserved in the corpus of ancient Norse writings which has come down to us relatively intact, despite its Christian editing. This *Elder Edda* was originally written down in medieval Iceland in an age quite different from that of archaic cataclysm. In the Edda, the cataclysm ends with the destruction of ancient culture, a change in religion, the destruction of the old gods and the casting out of humanity into a devastated and hostile world.

The antiquity of the story is emphasised in the *Voluspa*, in which the prophetess Vola calls it *"the ancient lore of men, the oldest that I know."* There is no mention of the use of iron in the story, and the time before Ragnarok is seen as an 'age of gold', a prosperous era of good climate and abundance. The whole sequence of events leading up to the flood seems well-considered, as if it were an historical account of an actual event. The catastrophe begins with a drought caused by the *"falling of fires from heaven."* Earthquakes follow: *"Then shall come to pass these tidings also"*, says *The Deluding of Gylfi*. *"All the earth shall tremble so, and the rocks, that the trees shall be torn up from the Earth, and the rocks fall to ruin; and all fetter and bonds shall be broken and rent... Then the sea shall gush forth upon the land, because the World Serpent stirs in giant wrath and advances upon the land.*" In another version, the Icelandic Skald (state poet) Arnor Jarkaskald writing in AD 1030, says: "*The bright sun becomes black; the Earth sinks into the sea.*"

The evidence for the actual ancient catastrophe was collected together by a German geologist, W. Wildvang. In 1911, his book *Eine prähistorische Katastrophe an der deutschen Nordseekuste* (A Prehistoric Catastrophe on the German North Sea Coast) revealed that in the course of innumerable drillings and peat-diggings, he had found evidence for a "*catastrophe of annihilating force*". With great violence, wrote Wildvang, "*the North Sea first rushed over our alluvial landscape up to the edge of the sandy area, and destroyed all vegetation with its saltiness, for this deluge was long-lived. Trees were knocked over by the first onrush of the water... the tops of uprooted trees always point to the east, which supports the contention that the cataclysm was caused by a westward storm.*"

About the middle of the thirteenth century BC, this deluge overwhelmed the German coast between the Ley and the Dollart. Similar observations of trees overwhelmed in the Fenlands of Cambridgeshire and Lincolnshire indicate a similar deluge, even to the observed consistent orientation of felled 'bog oaks'. In Germany, Wildvang found human skeletons among the debris of the catastrophe. Near Pilsum was the remains of a warrior with his shield, buried under six feet of sea mud. Other observations corroborated the contention that there had been a tidal wave. At the end of the last century the Kiel geologist E. Forchhammer noted traces of a great flood in his native Schleswig-Holstein. Sixty feet above mean sea level, Forchhammer found sea pebbles and shells. "*If we compare the results of these observations*" wrote Forchhammer, "*we must conclude that a deluge coming from the west once flooded these coasts, exceeding greatly in height and extent any other known to history.*" By examining the contents of Bronze Age graves and fields which were covered with the diluvial mud, archaeologists were able to date the deluge as having occurred in about 1220 BC.

Wildvang's catastrophe - the original Ragnarok - was followed by a severe climatic alteration: a fall in mean temperature of between three and four degrees Celsius (about 5 - 7 degrees Fahrenheit) The snow line of the Scandinavian mountains dropped from 6,250 feet to 4,950 feet, glaciers developed in the Alps where before they had been absent, and all over the world, glaciers began to advance. Precipitation, in general, increased, and between 1200 and 1000 BC boglands enlarged their areas. Cultural changes occasioned by the dis aster may have included the cessation of megalith building.

The cause of this 'climatic drop' is only ascribable to a massive volcanic eruption which caused a tsunami and pumped masses of volcanic ash into the Earth's atmosphere. When a similar event occurred in 1883 with the eruption of Krakatoa, the average temperature recorded worldwide dropped by two degrees Celsius (3.6 degrees Fahrenheit), leading to bad harvests and the rainy summer and snowy winter of 1885-6. Similar observations followed the Mount Saint Helens volcanic eruption of 1980 when vast amounts of ash were blasted into the upper atmosphere. In antiquity, such a disaster would have had a profound effect upon its survivors, who would have attributed it to the gods, and remembered it in enduring myths of world cataclysm.

13. In the 1950s, the British government built many new sea defences like this wall at Eccles, Norfolk. In the 1980s, to keep taxes low, United Kingdom policy was to 'let nature take its course', and to let the sea overwhelm the land rather than spend money on new defences.

Chapter 4
Atlantis and Other Sunken Civilisations

" . there were earthquakes and floods of extraordinary violence, and in a single dreadful day and night all your young fighting men were swallowed up by the Earth, and the island of Atlantis was likewise swallowed up by the sea and disappeared: this is why the sea in that area is to this day impassable to shipping, which is hindered by shoals just beneath the surface, the remains of a sunken island."   Plato: *Timaeus*

Although virtually every body of cultural tradition alludes to a universal deluge, those stories differ in one significant way from lost land legends: they tell that the deluge, though long-lasting, was temporary, and that the sub merged land finally emerged again to become dry and habitable. Tales of marine incursions are different, for the town or land, once deluged, is lost for ever. In the most famous version of the story, the submergence of Atlantis, a whole land or perhaps even a continent, is lost in a very short time, never to be seen again.

Atlantis has caught the imagination of every generation since the first time its tale was told, supposedly to Plato by Solon of Athens, who had himself received the legend from Egyptian priests at Sais. Controversy has raged ever since over whether Plato invented the story as an allegory of his perfect state, or whether there was indeed an arcane tradition handed down orally by the initiates of Sais. In his dialogues Timaeus and Critias, Plato gives detailed descriptions of the situation, form, geography, history, economics and politics of this fabulous land, stating that it was destroyed nine thousand years before his time.

Other authors have corroborated Plato's assertions about Atlantis, though critics of the concept have not been slow to point out that their concurrence may have been because they copied Plato's work. Plato himself claimed to have visited Sais in order to check Solon's story, and one of his disciples, Krantor, also came back to Greece with the same information. Krantor stated that he had seen the Egyptian inscriptions recording the history of Atlantis, but they have since been lost. An ancient Egyptian manuscript dating from 550 BC is said to exist today in a private library in Paris. Formerly the property of the author Pierre Benoit, it is supposed to have been the source for his celebrated novel *Atlantida*.

One of the problems of Atlantology is that of the name applied to the land. Often Greek writers called it by alternative names such as Poseidonia or Poseidonis, and the biographer Plutarch described a similar continent known as Ogygia, a land also mentioned in the writings of Homer.

The Roman historian Marcelinus, who lived in the fourth century of the Christian Era, described the swallowing-up of "*a large island*" in "*the Atlantic Sea*". This has always been identified as Atlantis, though it may equally be a record of the disintegration of islands on the coast of Britain, including parts of the Scillies, which probably went down during his lifetime. Thomas Short's *A General Chronological History of the Air*, etc. also records a Welsh earthquake in AD 394, and this may be connected with Marcelinus's observations.

Since the time of Plato, the existence of an historical Atlantis has been hotly disputed. Those believing in it cite the near-universal distribution of the universal flood myth. They conclude that these tales, whose features are so consistent despite their geographical separation, are unlikely to have originated independently, and are probably garbled folk memories of survivors of the Atlantean cataclysm, who were scattered in all directions. Another theory is that the legend itself was a well-known tale in Atlantis, and it has been handed down orally over countless generations to the present day. The relics of formerly

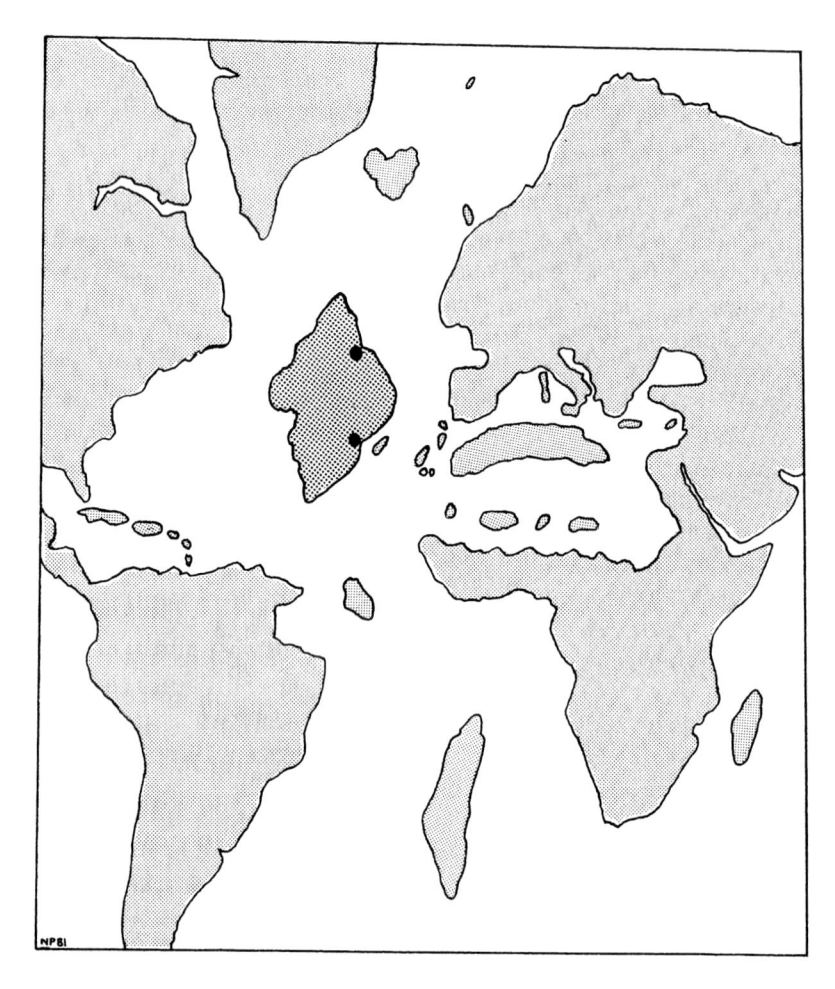

14. An interpretation of geography in the days of Atlantis, according to the London Lodge of the Theosophical Society around the beginning of the twentieth century.

advanced civilisations, such as the existence of advanced astronomical abilities in ancient Mexico and ancient Britain, have also been interpreted as the remains of an Atlantean science.

The dating of the end of Atlantis is often a stumbling-block to believers in orthodox history, for to place an advanced civilisation 11,000 years before the present is to suggest a loss of technique that is not compatible with an implicit belief in the unbroken upward progress of mankind. Believers in the traditional image of Atlantis suggest that the evolution of stone tools visible in archaeological sequences shows a re-ascent towards civilisation following a collapse from a state of former advancement.

A few survivors, they argue, cast out from their civilised land into a barren and hostile post-cataclysmic world, would have been compelled to re-learn methods of survival; rather like a modern person used to the comforts of the electronic age suddenly cast away on the proverbial desert island. Their first attempts at stone and bone tools, they argue, would inevitably be clumsy and inept. The only part of the civilisation that would survive, if in albeit unintelligible terms, would be orally transmitted stories. Hence we get the Biblical legend of the Fall of Man, a casting-out of transgressors from a paradise into a wilderness; tales of a former worldwide magical technology, flying machines in antiquity, great cities and technological wonders the like of which have not been seen until the twentieth century.

Although heartily disputed by some geologists, there is evidence that the mid-Atlantic - the traditional site for Atlantis - formerly contained land. When telegraphic cables were being laid across the ocean in 1898, there was a breakage 500 miles north of the Azores. Grapples were used to recover the cable from the abyss, and in pulling up the wires, fragments of rock were also recovered from the ocean floor. When examined, geologists confirmed that the rock was a volcanic lava of a type that had cooled and solidified in air. The volcano producing the lava had been on dry land.

During a more recent survey of the ocean bed, cores recovered from the depths revealed the frustules (skeletal remains) of the microscopic aquatic plants known as diatoms. When examined by physiological experts, these proved to belong to species that are known to be exclusively freshwater in habitat, showing again that at this mid-Atlantic location there had at some time been land with freshwater rivers or lakes. In 1956 Dr Rene Malaise of the Riks Museum, Stockholm, announced that he and his colleague, Dr P.W. Kolbe, had dated these deposits to between ten and twelve thousand years before the present the era ascribed to Atlantis by Plato.

Atlantis has, of course, attracted more than its fair share of studies from occultists of all persuasions. Psychics, ritual magicians, occult historians and recipients of arcane lore (of uncertain derivation and veracity) have all written at length on the lost continent. Some have even claimed that Atlantis, far from being the fount of all civilisation, was a degenerate successor of a more lofty and accomplished one originally sited in Lemuria or Mu. According to the theosophical researches of James Churchward, Mu was located in the Pacific Ocean at an unimaginably distant era in the past, and was the origin-point of all human culture.

According to Churchward, all surviving mythology, symbolism and religions are understandable only in terms of Muvian civilisation. In his books on various aspects of the legendary continent, Churchward expounded his philosophy which, he claimed, came from esoteric Tibetan writings aided by his own inspired interpretation of a curious collection of pre-Columbian Mexican inscriptions. The existence of this collection - which Churchward calls *"Niven's Mexican Tablets"* has long been in contention, for it is by no means certain whether they actually existed outside of Churchward's writings; or, if they did exist, whether the cryptic hieroglyphs engraved upon them were indeed as Churchward represented them and interpreted them.

From these mysterious tablets, Churchward claimed to have reconstructed the ancient language, history, religion, symbolism and evolutionary history of the Muvian world. Mu, he asserted, had sunk beneath the waves all of 50,000 years ago - a lavish time-scale that has much in keeping with the panoramic vistas of history found in Indian cosmology and their Theosophical derivatives. According to Churchward, the Muvian catastrophe occurred when subterranean pockets of gas ignited or caused subsidence on a continental scale; a fascinating theory, recently resurrected by proponents of alternative energy sources.

The link with Mexico seems compatible with possible evidence on both sides of the Atlantic and the Pacific, for 'lost civilisation' writers like Ignatius Donnelly and James Churchward have claimed that Mexico became the repository of the knowledge and culture lost when either Mu or Atlantis went down. Of course it cannot have been both! Churchward's other source, Tibet, is in the mainstream of theosophical tradition; for the teachings of theosophy state that at the destruction of Atlantis a branch of the Aryan race (which, Madame Blavatsky and her followers assure us, had evolved in Atlantis), fled to the Himalayas, where they descended beneath the mountains to found vast and impregnable underground cities.

Traditionally known as Shambhalla and Agharthi, these cities traditionally are the abode of the World Wise Men or White Lodge, a group of near-immortal Atlantean adepts whose psychic powers still direct the affairs of history. By a quirk of history, those arch believers in Atlantis, the Nazis sent expeditions to bleak and distant Tibet during World War II to attempt to enlist the support of the 'cosmic masters' of Agharthi. Churchward's exposition of the origin of the swastika - an important sacred symbol in both Mexico and Tibet, and crucial to many Atlantean diffusionist theories - were, with good reason, almost identical with those publicised by Professor Hermann Wirth, author of *Die Heilige Urschrift der Menschheit* (1932-1936). Whatever the truth about Atlantis and Mu - and the evidence for Atlantis is much more compelling than that for the Pacific continent - it is certain that these legends of lost lands will continue to exercise a considerable hold over peoples' minds.

Everything mysterious in this world has a legend that serves to explain it. From the simplest superstitions of unlearned people to the most complex hypotheses of scientific research, stories and ideas are advanced seeking to explain the reasons and causes of events. Every mysterious place, whether it be a natural outcrop of rock, a lake, a cave or an unusual combination of topographic features, has its associated folk mythology. One common strand which links these tales is the recurrence of certain motifs for specific classes of place. This phenomenon has long been known by students of folklore, who, in their meticulous research have listed and detailed each and every known variant in massive volumes of impeccable scholarship.

Nostalgia for a lost golden age is a perennial human emotion, and when evidences of that former age are still visible, it is inevitable that legends will grow up around them. The memory of coastal towns overwhelmed by the sea has naturally given rise to several legends which occur in similar form all around the coasts of northern Europe. One of these is the ghostly bells that may be heard tolling out to sea during stormy weather. These spectral bells are invariably believed to be the bells of churches inundated by the waves, stirred again into action by the force of the water. This attractive theory falls down because every church lost to the sea was first destroyed by wave action, invalidating the slightest possibility that bells could still hang in a submarine belfry. Only in recent years have churches been flooded in that manner, when the damming of valleys for water reservoirs or hydro-electric schemes have literally buried whole villages beneath standing water. No doubt modern tales of tolling bells are attached to these places, for several lakes, including that at Bala in Wales, have 'drowned bells' stories.

During the Middle Ages, it was commonly believed that ringing church bells during storms would quell the demons causing the storm and thus prevent damage to persons, property and land. The sound of a bell was deemed sufficient to still tempestuous seas, for the bell at Heighington church, Durham, is inscribed in Latin to St Peter: "T*hou Peter, when struck, calm the angry waves.*" Bells were believed to possess miraculous powers, being part of the worldwide practice of suppressing the demonic empire by means of sound. From fireworks to gongs, rattles, whistles, crackers, chanting, mantras, sutras and hymns, sound has always proved efficacious in quelling undesirable psychic states. Bells were believed to prevent lightning, suppress demons and affect all manner of other phenomena. At Dorchester Abbey, for example, the tenor bell was reputed to have the power of killing snakes by its sound alone, and in recent times, Nazi occultists are said to have pondered the properties of the bells of Oxford, which were reputed to have warded off a German air raid.

The legends connected with 'drowned bells' may have an origin totally unconnected with inundated coastal churches for the German geomantic researcher Wilhelm Teudt discovered that the early Christian church considered bells to be Pagan instruments of the Devil. Christian missionaries, asserted Taudt, confronted with Pagan bells, would cast them into lakes or rivers to 'drown' their influence, nullifying their supposed harmful powers. Later, when the Christians realised the efficacy of bells, they merely 'baptised' them in water, converting them to the service of Christ. Tales of drowned tolling bells may therefore be folk-memories of the practices of the first Christians in these islands.

At Tostherne Mere in Cheshire, we find one such 'drowned bell' legend. There, a church bell is supposed to have fallen into water whilst being transported to a new site. The rope broke when a profane workman uttered a blasphemous oath. According to tradition, every Easter Sunday a mermaid comes up a subterranean channel from the Mersey just to ring the bell. In the same county, at Combermere, the lake was said to hold an Abbey bell, stored at Wrenbury after the dissolution of the monasteries. It, too, sank beneath the waves when a workman blasphemed in the boat ferrying the bell across the mere.

A Christian reversal of Teudt's bell-drowning rituals is found in a tale told at Bosham in Sussex. There, in a creek in front of the church, is a place called the Bell Hole. Local lore asserts that in the Hole lies the tenor bell of the church, taken away by Danish

15. Bosham Church, Sussex, location of a bell-ringing legend.

raiders in the tenth century. As the Vikings rowed away with their booty, including the bell, the monks of Bosham rang their other bell to tell the villagers that it was now safe to return to their looted homes. Hearing her sister bell, the tenor bell joined in the peal. This vibration capsized the Danish craft and drowned the Pagans. It is said that to this day the drowned bell joins in whenever the church's peal is sounded.

Even today, local newspapers in coastal regions occasionally carry reports of people hearing "spectral bells". This phenomenon is usually dismissed as being the sound of bell buoys carried over unusually long distances by freak weather conditions, yet their continuity with age-old lore suggests more. Whatever the origin of the sounds, the story is widespread, being attached to the lost churches of Shipden near Cromer in Norfolk, Selsey in Sussex, the Welsh Lost Lowland Hundred, the Cornish coast of Lyonesse, Kilgrimod off Blackpool in Lancashire, and Ravenser on the Holderness coast of Humberside. Usually, hearing the bells produces no evil effects, but the Rocks of Minquiers to the south of the Channel Island of Jersey has the legend that any mariner who hears the spectral bells there knows that he is sailing his last voyage, and will die before reaching land. The ship's bell itself was universally acknowledged to be the embodiment of the ship's soul and the harbinger of bad tidings. At Lloyd's of London, the Lutine Bell is still sounded prior to the announcement of a ship lost at sea or of a satellite in space.

Another legend commonly found associated with lost lands is that of the floodgate guardian who, through drunken ness, fails in his duty to close the gates. The sea then comes in, and the land is overwhelmed. In the Welsh lost Lowland Hundred of Cantref y Gwaelod, the guardian Seithenyn was responsible for the disaster and at the Breton city of Ker Ys, a demonic figure seduces the king's daughter into stealing the flood-gate keys from her father, with disastrous results. In both cases, the flood ing is seen as divine retribution for the licentiousness of the inhabitants.

16. The Japanese daimyolin hammers the rivet rock into the head of the earthquake catfish.

The Welsh Triads record a legend of a deluge which is related both to the universal flood myth and also the more local destruction of Lyonesse. This great deluge is counted as one of the Three Catastrophes of Britain, the other two being extermination by fire and obliteration through drought. The great flood was caused when Llyn Llion, the Lake of Waves, overflowed the whole land, and everyone was drowned save the twin brothers Dwyfan and Dwyfach in their coracle. Another version of this tale recounts that the vessel Nefyddnaf-Nefion carried a pair of each living species. This great lake of Llyn Llion, whose name closely resembled that of the lost lands of Lyonesse and Leasowe the Cornish and Wirral lost lands, was reputed to contain a ferocious monster called the Addanc. This Addanc was caught by Hu the Mighty and dragged from the lake Ychain Banog, the Horned Oxen, and the lake never again overflowed.

In Norse mythology, the equivalent of the Addanc was the Midgardsorm or World Serpent, which girdled the ocean bed. This Midgardsorm was believed to be the source of all earthquakes, and hence the tidal waves that caused inundations. Its concept is very advanced, for the serpentine mid-oceanic ridges from which most earth-movements originate, straddle the world as might a World Serpent. The god Thor attempted to catch the Midgardsorm using an ox-head as bait, but failed, and at Ragnarok it burst forth, along with the rest of the demonic empire destined to destroy the gods and the Earth. In Japan, where appaling earthquakes happen regularly, this flood-causing serpent was portrayed as a catfish, and it was the job of the god-superior of the Kashima Shrine to order the daimyojin to drive down the 'rivet-rock of the World' upon the earthquake namazu (catfish) to ward off future earthquakes.

Just as an earthquake can be traced to a source or epicentre, so the origins of massive floods were attributed to one specific, if stereotypical, place. Perhaps this is the last vestige of an ancient understanding of seismology? Legends of deluge waters rising from a single source are found in the Koran. There, it was an oven which began to bubble and overflow water all around it at the commencement of the Noachian flood. The tradition stemmed

17. Two medieval representatives of the Migardsorm, the World Serpent of the Northern Tradition. Left: Thor fishing for the Midgardsorm on a stone from Gosforth, Cumbria; Right: Medieval drawing of the Orm, with Thor's ox-head bait.

from the Mazdean legend of Persis which asserted that the waters issued from a woman's oven. In Welsh tradition, this overflowing vessel was situated on the banks of the River Severn which geomorphologists have shown to be once a drowned valley, having suffered massive subsidence and over flow. Irish mythology tells that the flood's origin-point was a barrel, opened in curiosity by a foolhardy woman, a parallel with the celebrated Greek legend of Pandora, the mother of Pyrrha, the female flood survivor.

Every schoolchild has been told the tale of King Canute and his throne on the sea shore. Like Alfred's burnt cakes, it has overwhelmed all of the more important events in the monarch's life. There are two common versions of the Canute story, both involving the tide. In the first, Canute deliberately sets up his throne on the shore in order to impress upon his obsequious courtiers that he is not omnipotent. He orders the advancing tide to stop, but Canute's regal imperatives of course have no effect and he gets wet. The sycophantic courtiers are then lectured that only God is all-powerful, an object lesson in human vanity. The other version makes Canute the vain one, believing that as the divine monarch he has power over the waves. As in the first version, he finds himself overwhelmed by the tide, and this time it is he who goes away chastened.

Historians consider both stories apocryphal, but it has never been pointed out that the story probably originates in an incident recounted in Snorri Sturluson's *Heimskringla*. Sturluson, to whom we are forever indebted for committing the Norse holy book *The Edda* to paper, compiled *Heimskringla* from the various sagas of the Norse kings, a mixture of traditional and semi-mythological tales and historical record up to the year 1177.

From the *Saga of St Olav* we find an account of the event which probably became garbled into the Canute legend. During the almost interminable wars that ravaged Scandinavia during the eleventh century, Canute, king of England and Denmark, was ravaging Norway. King Olav and King Anund, allies against Canute, *"took counsel together and decided that King Olav and some of his men should go upon land right through the woods to the place where the water of the River Helgea (Holy River) ran down. There at the outlet of the river they made a dam of trees and turf and so blocked the water; in addition they dug dikes and brought the waters together so that there was a great flood."*

Having dammed up these waters, the Norwegians waited for Canute and his army, whom they knew would berth for the night at the river's mouth. When Canute's fleet had dropped anchor there for the night, "*King Olav then had the dam broken down and so brought the river back into its original course... in the morning when it was light, many of their men were on land, some talking, others playing games. They had word of nothing before the waters were rushing down on them in torrents. Then followed great trees which drove out against their ships, damaging them, and waters flooding all the meadows. The men on land were drowned and so were many on board ship; but all who could manage it severed their ropes and cast themselves loose, and then the ships were driven into one another. The great Dragon, on which was the king himself, was driven out by the flood...*" Canute's invasion was repulsed by a man-made flood, so perhaps the 'throne on the beach' story is more of an allegorical joke at Canute's expense than historical fact.

Canute's legendary throne was set up on the foreshore between high and low tide marks. This area, being neither land nor sea, and hence part of the vague terrain of boundaries, has several traditions. The masonic oath, for example, warns that he who divulges the awesome secrets of the Craft shall be torn asunder and buried on the foreshore between the tide marks. The mutineer Richard Parker, who ran up the Red Flag on his ship during the Nore Mutiny in 1797, was hanged for his offense. After his execution, his body was buried between the tide marks as his punishment for treason and heresy.

At Whitby, the ancient tradition of constructing the 'Penny Hedge is observed. There, a 'hedge' or fence of brushwood, traditionally cut with a knife costing a penny, is made on the foreshore between high and low water marks. The 'hedge' must be strong enough to withstand three tides. During its construction, the Town Crier had to recite an account of the crime which led to the imposition of the 'hedge-making' penance. Five aristocrats, out hunting, had chased a stag, which took refuge in a peasant's hut. The peasant, devoutly at prayer, refused to allow them to kill the stag and thus profane the holy hour. Enraged, the hunters broke down the door and put the peasant to the sword.

Even though the murder of peasantry by noblemen was not considered a serious crime by the state, the Church excommunicated the murderers, who could not be re-admitted to the sacrament before a penance was paid. This was granted by the Abbot of Whitby in the form of the 'Penny Hedge'. Originally, the hedge was made by representatives of the five families, but later, after payment of a considerable sum to the Abbey, the penitence was allowed to be delegated. The penitential 'hedge', with its connotations of the Canute legend and the practice of burying murderers and heretics on the foreshore, may represent a garbled memory of former boundaries now lost to the sea.

Of all the curiosities associated with lost lands, perhaps the weirdest is an event which took place on August 9th, 1888. On that day, the tug, *Victoria* left Great Yarmouth for a sea trip to Cromer. On the return journey, she struck the submerged ruins of Shipden church and was wrecked with considerable loss of life. Of all the foreshore legends, this is the only instance of a church sinking a ship; and it actually happened!

When the oil tanker Torrey Canyon ran aground on the Seven Stones Reef off Land's End in 1967, causing one of the first major oil spills on the British coast, press reports announced that it had struck the reputed remains of the lost land of Lyonesse. This submerged tract, otherwise called Ermonie or Parmenia, was perhaps the most famed and the most extensive of the lost lands of Britain, a former province of the ancient Kingdom of Dumnonia which figures in the corpus of legends known as The Matter of Britain. According to Cornish tradition, the land of Lyonesse was fertile and prosperous, possessing a number of

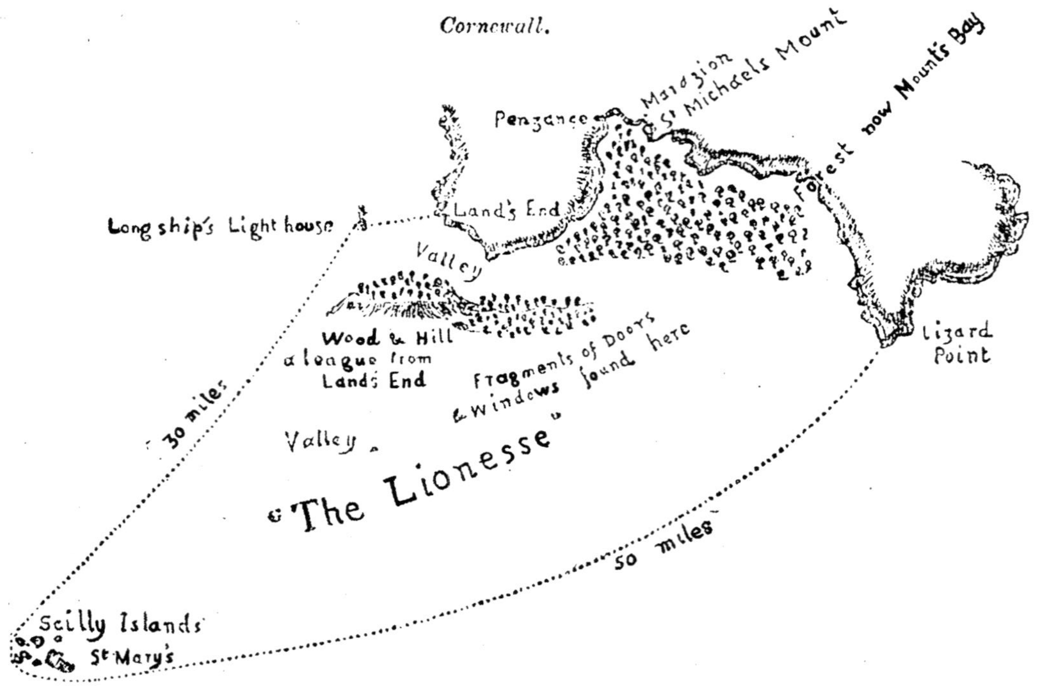

18. Dame Agnes Strickland's map (c. 1900) of Lyonesse.

towns and no. fewer than 140 churches. The final apocalypse which eliminated this vast territory was, according to the story, a sudden and final cataclysm. Possibly as the result of an underwater earthquake which lowered the level of the land suddenly and drastically, a huge wave-front swept across Lyonesse, destroying all in its wake. In common with many myths of flood and inundation, there was but one survivor, n this case named Trevilian. This Trevilian rode on horseback ahead of the advancing tsunami to reach high ground and safety. After his lucky escape, he became the founder of the Cornish Trevelyan family, whose coat of arms bears, in commemoration of the event, a horse coming out of water.

Although the tradition of Lyonesse is well known, what evidence is there for its reality? The antiquary Camden asserted that Land's End once undoubtedly stretched far to the west of its present termination, extending to the south and west and connecting with the present Scilly Isles, which are held by locals to be the dry hilltops of an inundated land. A map of Lyonesse, prepared by Agnes Strickland and published in Beccles Willson's 1901 book Lost England, shows a territory with a coastline about 80 miles in length. It includes a "*wood and a hill a league from Land's End*", a valley between this and Land's End itself, and a large forest in the present Mount's Bay by St. Michael's Mount.

It is an established fact that the famed promontory of St Michael's Mount, which is now cut off from the mainland by the sea at high tide, was once not merely connected to the land, but was several miles from the coast. The chronicler William of Worcester asserts that the Mount was formerly five or six miles from the sea, and surrounded by a very dense wood. This story is borne out by the Cornish name for the holy hill, Carreg los en cos - variously anglicised as *Carreg Luz en Kuz, Carey Cowse in Clowse*, and *Carreg Coedh yn Clos* - meaning 'the Grey Rock in the Wood', which is certainly a misnomer for its present situation. Documentary evidence for its former position exists in the *Domesday Book*, compiled in 1086. In the section dealing with Cornvalge (Cornwall), we find the following: "*The land of St Michael. Keiwal holds the church of St Michael. Brismar was*

19. Stone 'hedge' on the shore below high water in the Isles of Scilly.

holding the Danish tax. The land is 8 Caracutes. There is one Caracutes with one villan, and two borderii and 10 acres of pasture. Value 20 shillings."

There is no reference to the "Land of St Michael" being an island. Where islands existed at the time of Domesday, they were invariably recorded as such, as, for example, the Isle of Wight and Portland. What makes the Domesday entry important is that it records the territory as thirty times its present extent. In eleventh-century metrology, four virgates equal a hide, 30 acres to a virgate. Eight caracutes were equivalent to 480 acres. The present land area of the Mount is under 30 acres, against the former extent of the lands at about 1440 acres in all. With its Cornish name ('The Grey Rock in the Wood'), and the evidence of *Domesday*, we do not have to look far for other evidence that the sea's advance has obliterated most of the area. In Mount's Bay formerly existed the remains of a 'submarine forest' - the roots and stumps of trees which had grown on land which is now below sea level. Observers considered the appearance of the stumps in situ as the result of a vast and sudden subsidence rather than a gradual erosion of the shore, a contention given credence in both local tradition and local topography.

The 'drowning' of Mount's Bay is just one instance of a phenomenon visible all round the south-western promontory of Britain, once known as Dumnonia or West Wales. There, the estuaries of rivers appear to be filled with water to a far greater height than they were at the period when they were formed. The estuaries of the Exe, Tamar, Fal and Dart all share this characteristic, and submerged forests have been reported at many sites along the coast.

In his *Report on Cornwall*, Sir Henry de la Beche remarked that "*submarine forests are so common that it is difficult not to find traces of them in the district at the mouths of all the numerous valleys which open upon the sea and are in any manner silted up.*" "*If we turn to the Bristol Channel,*" asserted the eminent geologist Sir Charles Lyell, "*we find that both on the north and the south sides of it there are numerous remains of submerged forests; ... one of those at Porlock Bay... extends far from the land. There is good reason to believe that there was once a woodland tract uniting Somersetshire and Wales, through the middle of which the ancient Severn flowed."* This estuary of the Severn is in reality the largest 'drowned valley' in Britain. The outline of it has been somewhat modified by tidal action, and erosion continues at several sites. The island of Steep Holm in the centre of the Bristol Channel, as the Severn estuary is known, currently of interest as a strategic point in the erection of a proposed barrage across the Channel, was in the last century several times larger than it is today, and was regularly used for the pasturing of sheep.

Further evidence for the lost land of Lyonesse can be found in the Scilly Isles, the reputed upland of the territory. Local tradition asserts that the Scillies were once an integral part of the British mainland, and both the physical and documentary evidence indicates that this is indeed possible. In Roman times, the Scillies comprised but one major island. Writing in AD 240, Solinus called it Siluram Insulam - the Scilly Isle - as did Sulpicius Severus, in about 400 AD. According to the geographer Strabo, the number of isles in the whole Scilly group did not exceed ten, yet there are over 140 today. In AD 387, the Emperor Maximus banished a heretic to Sylina Insula, the Scilly Isle.

In his *Survey of Devon*, the antiquary Risdon wrote *"That region which geographers account the first of all Britain, and shooteth out farthest to the west, was once reputed the fourth part of this island, and supposed to be a kingdom before the sea swallowed up the land between St Burian and the islands of Scilly, included under the name of Danmonia."* Assertions such as this, and references in ancient writings, encouraged the Cornish antiquary William Borlase to undertake his own investigation of the story. After a visit to the Scillies in 1753 he wrote: *"The continual advances which the sea makes on the low lands are obvious... the flats which stretch from one island to another are plain evidences of a former union subsisting between many now distinct islands... the flats between Trescau, Brehar, and Sampson·are quite dry at a spring tide, and men easily pass dryshod from one island to another over sandbanks, where, on the shifting of the sands, walls and ruins are frequently dis covered, on which at full sea there are ten or twelve feet of water."* Borlase saw stone walls (known in Cornwall as 'hedges') *"descending from the Hill, and running many feet under the level of the sea towards Trescow."* At Annet, "The sand being washed away a few years since by some high tides" wrote Borlase," *discovered the walls of a house."*

Borlase's scientific observations were followed up in sub sequent years by others who wished to determine the reality of the Lyonesse legend. In 1794 the house remains at Annet were re-examined by a Mr Troutbeck. On March 16th, 1926, O.G.S. Crawford, one of the most eminent archaeologists of the twentieth century, visited the Samson Flats in order to examine some submerged stone 'hedges' - prehistoric walls delimiting former fields. His interest was aroused because these walls had been cited as evidence, he later wrote in his magazine Antiquity, that the legend of Lyonesse was historically true. If the present sea level were to be lowered by 60 feet, asserted Crawford, then the present Scilly archipelago would coalesce to form one major island - the *Siluram Insulam* of Solinus.

Having examined the walls, and found them to be authentic relics of a lost land, Crawford concluded that "there are good reasons for believing that the substance of the legend is true". However, he poured cold water on the romantics by asserting that the legend had arisen from observations of these 'hedges' between the Scilly islands, not from any orally-transmitted record of a cataclysm. He concluded that the Scillies had indeed once been a single large island, but that any connections between that island and the Cornish mainland were not proven.

Sceptical archaeologists at once claimed that the stone 'hedges' must have been fish-weirs, but this contention is easily dismissed as the walls do not follow marine contours, the essential characteristic of fish-weirs. The stone walls run from the land surface, down the beach and into the sea, proving beyond any shadow of doubt that there has been a major readjustment of the relative levels of land and sea since the walls were erected.

Stone walls are not the only remains to be found below high water mark in the Scillies. In 1934 Tebbutt excavated a stone cist on the shore of the central 'waist' of Old Man, now breached by the sea. The cist yielded Romano-British brooches of an unusual type. Off Tean, seven feet below mean sea level, Tebbut dis covered the remains of two stone "huts". Excavations of the remains of other stone buildings, wells and burial cists below the high water mark were carried out during the 1950s and 1960s at Great Arthur, Little Arthur, Tresco and St Martin's by Professor Thomas and his associates. Their conclusions were that the mean sea level relative to the land must have been at least 14 feet lower than at present.

In addition to the Scillies, the Seven Stones Reef has been cited as part of Lyonesse. There, according to tradition, was the land's capital, the City of Lions. "*About the middle way, between Land's End and Scilly*", recounts Gibson's edition of *Camden's Britannia*, "*there are rocks called in Cornish Lethas, by the English Seuen Stones, and the Cornish call the place within the stones Tregas (a dwelling), where, according to reports, windows and such other stuff have been taken up with hooks. It is said also that from Land's End to Scilly is an equal depth of water...*"

Sir Richard Carew, a contemporary of Sir Walter Raleigh, was a firm believer in Lyonesse. "*The space between the Land's End and the Isles of Scilly*", he wrote, "*being about thirty miles, to this day retaineth that name (Lyonesse), in Cornish Lethowsow, and carryeth continually an equal depth of forty to sixty feet, a thing not usual in the sea's proper dominion, save that about the midway there lieth a rock which at low water discovereth his head. They term it the Gulf, suiting thereby the other name of Scilla. Fishermen also casting their nets thereabouts have drawn up the pieces of doors and windows.*"

All the evidence of geologists, antiquaries and archaeologists points to a permanent incursion of the sea having taken place at some time after the Roman period but before the end of the Middle Ages. Carew's note on the sixty-foot depth of the sea between the Scillies and Crawford's assertion - that the sea level would have to be sixty feet lower in order for the Scillies to be one island - seem too concurrent to be chance. The submerged coastline of the former Dumnonia, complete with its drowned valleys and forests, indicates that some kind of major subsidence, perhaps as the result of an earthquake, must have occurred. *"The slow advances and depredations of the sea will by no means suffice"* wrote Borlase, to explain the changes apparent in the Scillies. The only solution to the problem, he believed, involved *"encroachments of the sea, and as manifest a subsidence of the land"*.

Borlase's ideas may have been conditioned by an earthquake he actually experienced. On July 15th 1757 at 6.30 pm., a major seismic shock was felt throughout Cornwall and as far away as the Scillies. In his report on the earthquake, which incidentally was the first scientific paper ever written on the phenomenon, Borlase located the epicentre at Penzance. Its extent - covering the region of the lost land of Lyonesse - shows that there is nothing inherently unlikely in a larger earthquake causing coastal inundation; for the 1757 earthquake is not the only one ever recorded in the area. *The Gentleman's Magazine* in 1799 reported another major earthquake in the same seismic zone, on the Channel Island of Guernsey, and many other earthquakes are known to have occurred in western Britain.

The date of the inundation of Lyonesse is usually reckoned at sometime in the sixth century of our era, perhaps concurrently with the similar destruction along the Coast of Wales, where the lost Lowland Hundred known as Cantref y Gwaelod was overwhelmed by the sea. It is possible that the Breton coast also suffered a similar fate, with the destruction of Caer Ys (Ker Ys), for to this day the stone circle at Er Lanic in Brittany is partially submerged by the tide. Some of the Cornish coastline, however, has been inundated in a more common manner, and eroded during storms. This process doubtless accounted for the lands around St Michael's Mount. Lyonesse, referred to in Arthurian legend, was certainly obliterated before the Saxon Conquest of Dumnonia, for when in AD 932, Howel, the last Cornish king, was forced to surrender his territory east of the Tamar to King

Athelstan of England, his subjects were referred to no longer as Britons, but as Cornwallians, from *com*, a horn or promontory. Had Lyonesse still existed, the name Cornwall, in Cornish *Kernow*, would have been meaningless.

Since the obliteration of Lyonesse, a continued process of attrition has claimed further land. During the eleventh century, major storms accounted for the loss of considerable portions of territory. The Anglo-Saxon Chronicle records for the year 1014; *"And on this year, on St Michael's Mass Eve, came a great sea-flood over this land, and ran up so far as never before, and submerged many towns, and mankind innumerable in number."* At Martinmas 1099, one of the worst floods on record took place: the chronicler Florence of Worcester recorded it thus: *"the sea came out upon the shore, and buried very many men and towns, and innumerable oxen and sheep"*. The Anglo Saxon Chronicle treats it as follows: *" 1099: This day also, on St Martin's Mass Day, sprang up the exceeding sea-flood, and did so much harm, being at a new moon."* It is possible that the 1099 flood, which is also reputed to have destroyed the land of which the Goodwin Sands are now the remains, and caused the formation of Mount's Bay which turned St Michael's Mount into an island.

Whatever the historical reality, Lyonesse has long served as a source of literary inspiration, to quote Beccles Willson *"submerged in a torrent of picturesque inaccuracy"*. Arthurian romance, especially the tale of Tristram and Iseult, alludes to the lost land as if it then existed. Spenser, in his Faery Queen, refers to the land *"Out of the countrie wherein I was bred, The which the fertile Lionesse is hight..."*

Various re-tellings of Arthurian romance from the nineteenth and twentieth centuries, with more or less the same subject matter, but with fanciful additions, mention this lost land. The most unlikely memorials to this erstwhile territory were British steam locomotives, three of which bore the name Lyonesse. The first was a Great Western locomotive, which ran from the beginning of the twentieth century until the 1930s. Overlapping this engine's career was that of a Southern Railways locomotive,

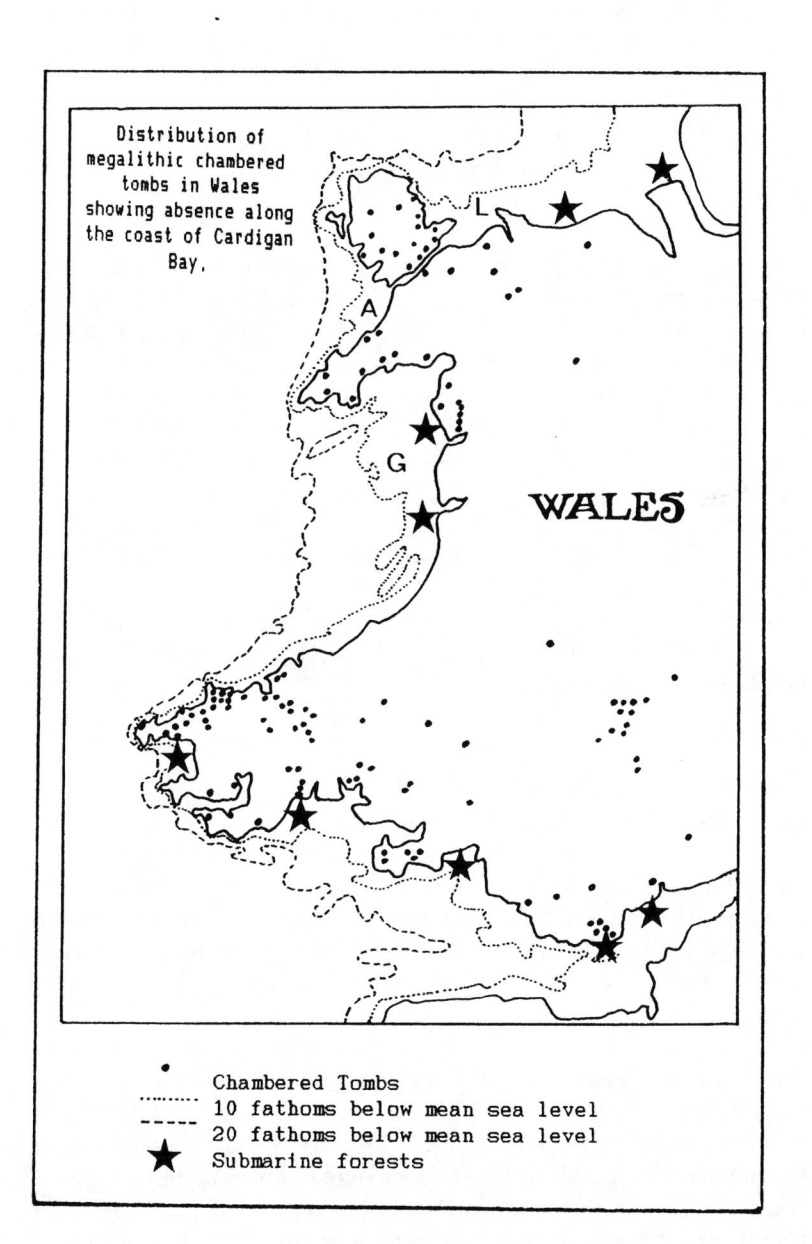

Distribution of megalithic chambered tombs in Wales showing absence along the coast of Cardigan Bay.

WALES

- • Chambered Tombs
- .... 10 fathoms below mean sea level
- ----- 20 fathoms below mean sea level
- ★ Submarine forests

one of a series which utilised names drawn from Arthurian legend. When the Southern engine was scrapped, its name passed to the final recipient- British Railways standard steam locomotive, number 73113 - built during the mid-1950s and itself scrapped ten years later. Unfortunately, there have been no more locomotives bearing this illustrious name.

The principality of Wales has lost more territory to the sea than other parts of Britain, and owing to its long unbroken culture, we have documentary evidence of the inundated lands. Manuscript number 3514 in the library of Exeter Cathedral, dated at about 1280, records *"There are three kingdoms that were submerged by the sea: The Kingdom of Tewthi, son of Gwynnon, King of Kaerrihog between Mynwy (St David's) and Ireland. No one escaped from it, neither man nor beast, except Teithi Hen and his horse, and for the rest of his life he was sick with fright. The second kingdom was that of Helig, son of Glannawg that was between Cardigan and Bardsey Island and as far as Mynwy. And that land was extremely good and fruitful and flat... and stretched from Aber [Aberystwyth] to Lleyn and as far as Aberdyfi. The sea submerged a third, the kingdom of Rhedfoe, son of Rheged..."*

Cantref y Gwaelod

Along the Welsh coast, then, we have a number of lost lands, each with their own recorded history. The largest of these, after Lyonesse, the largest tract of lost land in Britain, was the lost Lowland Hundred of Cantref y Gwaelod (sometimes rendered as Cantre'r Gwaelod), devastated by the sea, old Welsh chronicles assure us, sometime during the sixth century of the Christian Era.

This Cantref y Gwaelod was bounded by a sea wall, Sarn Badrig (St Patrick's Causeway), which extended for 22 miles from the coast of Merionethshire, half-way between Harlech and Barmouth. The coast between Sarn Badrig and Cardigan formed the north-eastern and southern boundary of the Lowland Hundred; the western limits ran between Cardigan and the

LOST WALES, WIRRAL & LANCASHIRE

CAER ARIANRHOD

LLYS HELIG

Legend:
- Lost Lands
- Limits of Ptolemy's map
- ● Lost Towns
- ■ Modern Towns

Labels on map: Lowscales, Aldingham, Singleton Thorpe, Kilgrimod, Waddon Thorpe, BELISAMA, SETEIA, Altmouth, TISOBIVS, Meols, Llys Helig, PRESTATYN, CHESTER, Caer Arianrhod, Caer Wyddno

Below: 1864 reconstruction of the realm of Helig ap Glannawg by lost lands researcher C.R. Hall.

MAP OF COAST OF NORTH WALES — Anglesey or Môn, Mouth of R. Ely, CARNARVON, DENBIGH, Supposed Ancient Coast Line

extremity of Sarn Badrig. The whole territory was fertile land, filled with many human settlements, the principal of which was Caer Wyddno, the city of Gwyddno Garanhir.

The geography of the Lowland Hundred is quite well documented. It was divided by four main roads which still exist as causeways visible at low tide: these are Sarn Bwch (the Goat's Causeway), which extends for about a mile and a half into the sea from the coast at Aberdysyni in Merionethshire- Sarn Cyngelyn (Cymbeline's Causeway) extending seven miles into the sea from Gwallawg; Sarn Ddewi (St David's Causeway), aligned upon the church of Llan Ddewi Aberarth (St David's) at the mouth of the River Arth; and Sarn Cadwgan (Cadogan's Causeway), half a mile from Sarn Ddewi, which runs into the sea for about a mile and a quarter. These roads, continuations of those on the present mainland, provided access to the main settlements of the Lowland Hundred. Caer Wyddno, for example, was reached by way of Sarn Cyngelyn.

According to legend, the last lord of the Lowland Hundred was Gwyddno Garanhir. Gwyddno maintained a grand court at Caer Wyddno, was a lover of culture and a brave warrior. Being a benevolent ruler, he took measures to combat the ever-present threat of an encroaching sea, and undertook the construction and maintenance of sea walls around the coast of E Cantref y Gwaelod. But although his most trusted men were put e in charge of the flood-gates controlling the estuaries, on a certain night, Seithenyn (sometimes known as Sicthenyn), one of the gate- masters, became drunk. Incapacitated by his alcoholic stupor, Seithenyn failed to carry out his duty, and the sea burst through with such force that the sea wall was washed away and the Hundred was inundated. According to legend, sixteen fortified towns were wiped out, and at least one thousand people drowned.

"The person mentioned as the main cause of the disaster", wrote Griffith Edwards in *Archaeologia Cambrensis* in 1849, was "*Seithenyn, son of Seithenyn Seidi, prince of Dyfed, or Dimetia, a part of South Wales.' The Triads*, a collection of ancient Welsh.

bardic poems, record: "*Seithenyn the Drunkard let in the sea over Cantre'r Gwaelod, so that all the houses and lands contained in it were lost. And before that time, there were found in it sixteen fortified towns, superior to all the towns and cities in Wales, except Caerllyon on the Usk. And Cantre'r Gwaelod was the dominion of Gwyddno king of Cardigan, and this even happened during the time of Ambrosius. And the people who escaped from that inundation came and landed in Arduduy, the country of Arvon, the Snowdon Mountains, and other places not before inhabited.*"

The Myvynan Archaeology contains some poems of the sixth or seventh century of the Christian Era that are commonly attributed to Gwyddno Garanhir. One is on the inundation of the Lowland Hundred, being couched in terms of a curse upon Seithenyn for his negligence in allowing the lands to be overwhelmed. According to tradition, Seithenyn ap Seithyn, unintentional destroyer of the Hundred, had many sons. Unlike their intemperate father, they became Christian holy men. The identities of Seithenyn's sons are shadowy, but the best documented is Arwystyl - otherwise Arwystyl Gloff ('The Lame') - who became a monk at Bangor Fawr in Maelor, on the banks of the River Dee, when the Hundred was destroyed, A similar tale is appended to the life of Helig ap Glannawg (or Glannog), whose lost land lay off the north coast of Wales.

With such a flourishing local lore and documentary evidence to go on, many antiquaries have attempted to find the material remains of Gwyddno's domain. Much of the area still becomes dry at low tide, especially during spring tides. Access to the Hundred may then be obtained by way of the sarnau, and many people have recovered fragments of building from the area over the years. Several maritime features, uncovered at low tide, still bear names associated with the time when they were on dry land. Three miles west of Aberaeron, about half a mile from the mean shoreline, is a bank of mud and stones called Eglwys y rhiw, 'the Church on the hillside'. As late as 1770 there were remains of human habitation reputed to be Caer Wyddno. William Owen Pughe wrote that "*three or four miles in the sea between the outlets of the rivers Ystwyth and Teivi... in the summer of 1770 I sailed over the ruins, on a very calm day and thus for about three minutes I had a clear view of them and many of the stones seemed to be large slabs and lying to confusion on the heap."* At the end of Sarn Badrig were sixteen large stones, possibly the remains of a megalithic structure.

This Sarn has been one of the main objects of interest to antiquaries seeking the remains of the Lost Hundred. Writing in the *Cambrian Register* is 1795, the Hengwrt antiquary Robert Vaughan asserted "*A whole Cantred or Hundred called Canter Gwaelod, stretching itself west and southwest about twelve miles in length... has been overwhelmed by the sea and drowned, and still a great stone wall, made as a fence against the sea, may be clearly seen... and is called Sarn Badrig, ie. St Patrick's Street or Bad-rwgg, ie. the boat or ship-breaking causeway.*"

"*Sarn Badrig,*" says Mr Bingley (cited by Griffith Edwards), "*is a stone wall which runs out into the sea from Mochras, a point of land a few miles to the south of Harlech, in a south-westerly direction, for nearly twenty miles; it is a wonderful work, being throughout twenty-four foot thick.*" Another researcher who travelled the coastline of Wales seeking lost lands was the Merseyside antiquarian and expert on sacred geometry Edward W. Cox. "*This causeway or embankment*" he wrote of Sarn Badrig, *"is now seen only at low tide, and there is no escaping the conviction if this be an artificial structure, which from this small portion I have been able to see, I think it is - that the legend is true. No one would build such a causeway fifteen feet below high water mark and the land must have subsided to bring it into its present condition. The fact that it retains its form, and has not been ruined or broken up, and removed piecemeal, also strongly tends to prove that subsidence and not erosion placed it beneath the sea.'*

For centuries, storms have been turning up the remains of inundated forests along that part of the Welsh coast. Giraldus Cambrensis asserted that St David's Head formerly extended much further into the sea, and that tree trunks bearing fresh

23. A submerged wall in Cardigan Bay. Drawing by Edward Cox, 1893.

marks of the axe were visible in his day. This theme was taken up by Camden, who wrote that in the time of Henry 11, storms laid bare the sandy shores of that coast, and *"the trunks of trees which had been cut down standing in the midst of the sea with the strokes of an axe as fresh as if they had been yesterday, with very black earth."* Later seekers of curiosities noted the phenomenon, but it was not until the nineteenth century that a scientific study of the sunken forest was undertaken. On November 7th, 1832, the Reverend James Yates read a paper titled *A Notice of a Submarine Forest in Cardigan Bay* before a meeting of the Geological Society of London. *"This forest,"* he said, *"extends along the coast of Merionethshire and Cardiganshire, being divided into two parts by the estuary of the Dovey, which separates those two counties. It is bounded on the land side by a sandy beach and a wall of shingles... Among the trees of which this forest consisted is the Pinus sylvestris or Scotch Fir; and it is shown that this tree abounded anciently in several Northern counties of England."*

All round the Welsh coast, traces of submerged forests have fascinated geologists and antiquaries alike. During the excavation for the Barry Docks in South Wales in 1884, John Storrie and F.T. Howard noticed many submerged levels of peat which had formerly been land. The building works for the Barry Extension Dock a year later brought to light a peat bed containing many fragments of woodland trees. In *The Quarterly Journal of the Geological Society*, A. Strahan listed the findings at Barry. The peat beds contained the remains of willow, fir, oak, sallow, hawthorn and hazel trees as well as bur-reeds. One oak piece found by John Storrie was five feet in length and ten inches in diameter, occurring in conjunction with a neolithic worked flint. Two prehistoric bone needles also turned up in the excavations.

Clement Reid, the Victorian authority on submarine forests, concluded that the lowest land surface represented a true forest growth such as could only live at an elevation clear of the highest tides, and that the land must have subsided at least 55 feet for it to have become submerged. Evidence for either a massive subsidence or an equally massive rise in sea level has been noted at many places, accounting for the 'sunken valleys' of Cornwall and the Bristol Channel. At Chepstow, the rock bed of the River Wye was found to be 42 feet below low water mark, showing a considerable subsidence. At the mouth of the River Dysyni on the shore of the Lost Lowland Hundred, oak trees up to six feet in diameter have been unearthed, showing that here, too, the subsidence was at least equal to that at Barry.

If the inundation of Cantref y Gwaelod was sudden, only an earthquake of massive proportions could have caused such a subsidence. Further north, evidence points to a gradual incursion of the sea, but in Cardigan Bay, like Lyonesse, a sudden flood is more likely. The date of this catastrophe has naturally prompted several estimates. Griffiths Edwards cited the year AM 3591 in the Jewish calendar and brought attention to the *Triads* passage *"in the time of Ambrosius"*, which would place it at the end of the fifth century AD.

Meyrick, in his *History of Cardiganshire* claims that the disaster occurred in the time of Gwrgant Farfdrwch - sometimes rendered as Gwrgan Varvtrwch - the king of Dumnonia who endowed Glastonbury Abbey in AD 601. The inundation certainly took place after the era of megalith building, for Margaret Davies has shown that along the coast between the estuaries of the Mawddach and the Teifi there are no megalithic remains whatsoever. Usually, major megalithic sites are characteristically only a few miles from the sea; but the same phenomenon can be observed along the coast of the Wirrall and South Lancashire, other areas with inundation traditions.

The dating of the Welsh losses can also be attempted from several early documentary sources. The Bard Taliesin, who lived at the end of the fifth and the beginning of the sixth century of the Christian Era, referred to the loss of Llys Helig (Helig's Palace) on the north coast of Wales as having taken place during the lifetime of his own contemporaries. The loss of Cantref y Gwaelod can be dated from entries in *The Black Book of Carmarthen* which gives the dates of Gwyddno Garanhir as 460 -

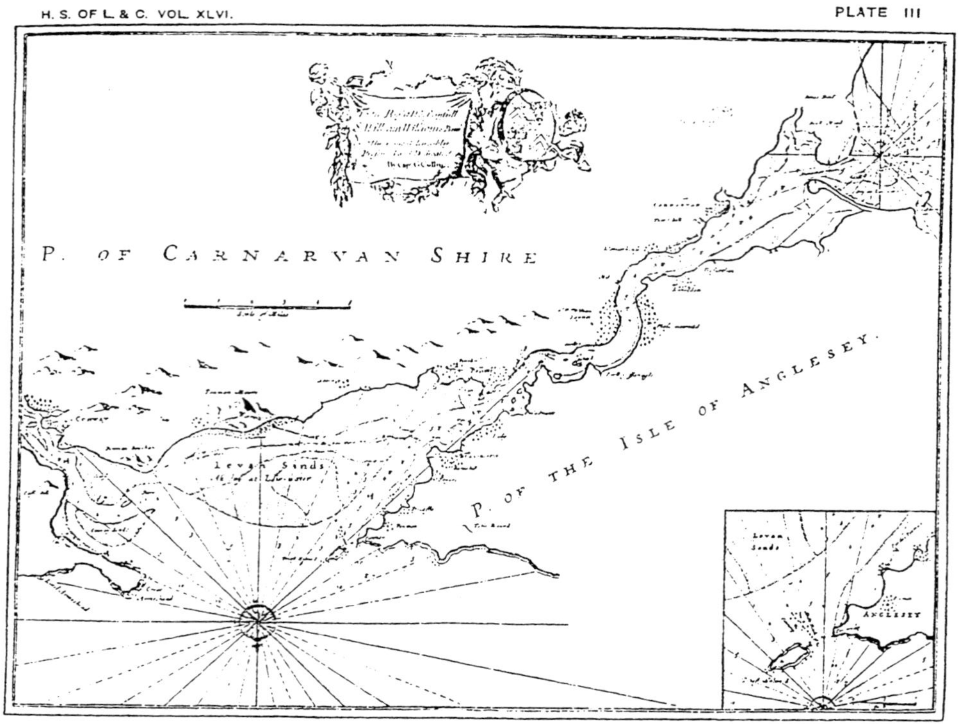

24. Collins's Hydrographic Chart, showing the Menai Straits, the location of Caer Arianrhod and Llys Helig.

520 AD. According to the Reverend F. Parry, the *Tulo Manuscript* says that Gwyddno's son was Elphin, patron of the Bard Taliesin.

In the Cantref y Gwaelod were Caer Cenedy ('The Camp of the Tribes'), Caer Wyddno (Gwyddno's city), and Cadair y Cedawl, ('The Chair of Cedawl'). *The Black Book* says: "*The Chair of Cedawl, God has overthrown.*" The interpretation of the cataclysm as God's punishment is a common reaction of the pious to natural disasters. Cedawl is traditionally supposed to have been an early Christian saint, but his name does not appear in any of the genealogies. It is possible that it is an alternative spelling for St Cedol, patron of Llangedol near Bangor. Cedol as an adjective means munificent or kind, an attribute that might be associated with an enlightened judgement-seat.

Caer Arianrhod

To the north of Cantref y Gwaelod, between the Lleyn peninsula and Anglesey, lay the fortress or town of Caer Arianrhod, "*a Roman fort down to its submergence in the 6th century*". The site of Caer Arianrhod is reputed to be a reef of stones lying in Caernarvon Bay half a mile from the present shoreline between Dinas Dinlle and the mouth of the River Llyfni. Its location was put on record in the map of Humphrey Llwyd, prepared in 1568 and published five years later, where the town is shown as Caer lerjenrhod. The name 'Arianrhod' comes from the ancient British Mother Goddess of the same name.

The history of the Caer is not as well documented as that of the Lost Lowland Hundred. The early medieval *Mabinogion Gacilent* refers to Arianrhod as being on land "now covered by the sea". *The Red Book of Hergest* calls it an existing caer, never a lost or submerged one, as it does Caer Wyddno, Llys Helig and Caer Cenedyr. Because this old Welsh book was certainly written before the overwhelming of Morfa Rhyanedd, the strip of land between the Great Orme's head and Conwy Bay, it gives us a clue to the chronology of Welsh land losses. Various antiquaries have sought Caer Arianrhod. According to Crofton Croker in his

Fairy Tales of Ireland, the site of the caer was rediscovered by the Welsh historian Dr Pughe. The Merseyside geomant Edward W. Cox refers to a "young artist" who visited the remains in 1890 or 1891 and "*made a drawing of part of them, and alleged that he found on some of the stones incised six-armed crosses.*" Writing in 1894, in the *Transactions of the Historic Society of Lancashire and Cheshire* [NS.vol X], Cox relates "About 25 years ago I went to Dwygyfylchi at the date of the lowest tide of the year, and with a good telescope I could see the long line of walls and buildings, covered with black seaweed." W. Ashton visited the site in 1909, and saw a "*crescent of stones... just below the surface of the water*". In 1913, F.C.Wynn drew a plan of the caer, having found concentric and rectangular enclosures of stone.

Tyno Helig

By far the best studied of the Welsh lost lands is the tract formerly known as Tyno Helig, or Helig's Vale. This territory was a low lying tract of land on the north coast of Caernarvonshire, stretching from Priestholm to Penmaenmawr and including part of Traeth Lafan, the present-day Lavan Sands. With an area reputed to be about twelve by eight miles in extent, Tyno Helig was ruled from Llys Helig, which stood, according to tradition, about half-way between the Great Orme's Head and Penmaenmawr. All that remains today of the land is the Lavan Sands, whose name means 'weeping', supposedly a lamentation over the loss of so much fertile land and so many inhabitants.

The Lavan Sands are exposed at low tides. They lie between Anglesey and the coast of North Wales. Here, the roots of trees have often been noticed when the water has ebbed with the spring tides. In the *Cambridge County Geography for Flintshire* (1914) we read "*In the fifth century there was a great inundation along the whole of the North Wales Coast, and the sea once more regained a large tract of land.*" The creation of the Lavan Sands by a great inundation appears to have taken place between the years AD 634 and 664. The whole episode is inextricably bound up with the fortunes of a local lord or sub-king named Helig ap Glannawg (or Glannog). According to local tradition, Helig ap

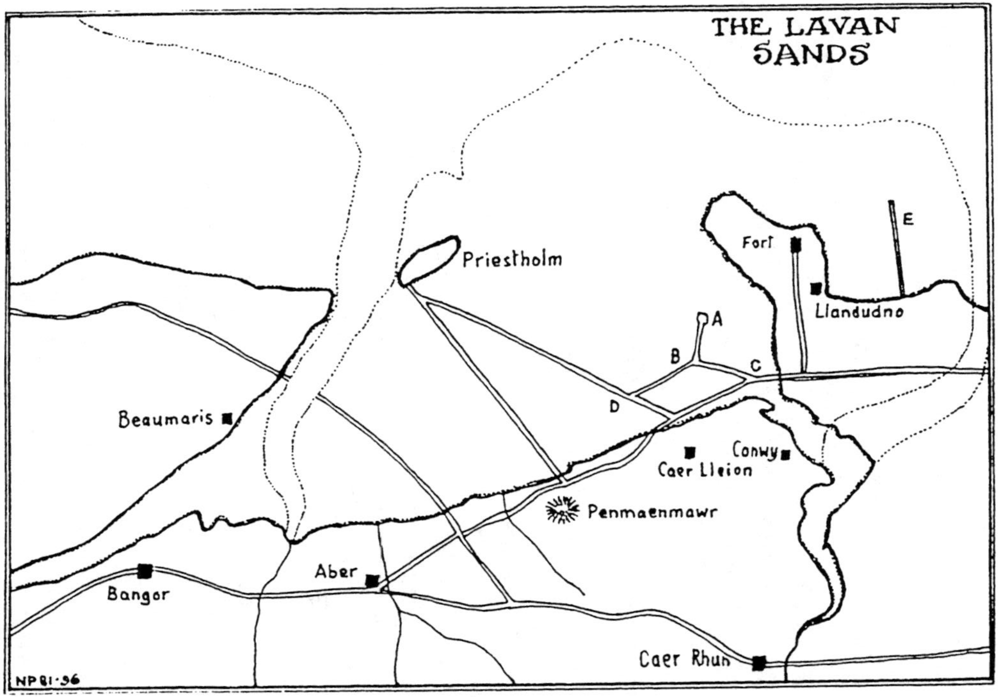

25. *The possible coastline of the Bangor - Llandudno region, at the time of the late Roman Empire. A: Bank of placed stones; B: Little Sarn; C: Castell Tremlydd; D: Llys Helig; E: Sarn Holland.*

Glannawg was lord of Abergele, Rhos, Arllechwedd, Llyn and Cantref y Gwaelod in addition to being Lord of Hereford. His palace, Llys Helig, was situated at the intersection of two important roads to the west of the present town of Conwy.

The Menai Strait which divides Wales from Anglesey did not exist at the time of Helig ap Glannawg, the western coastline of that island being roughly defined as at present by a wide estuary of the River Ogwen. The small island of Priest's Holm, which lies to the northwest of Anglesey, was an integral part of the coastline which stretched westward from the estuary to the Great Orme's Head. The River Conwy debouched into the Irish Sea by the Little Orme's Head, three miles northwest of its present estuary. Thus a tract of land, almost ten miles by seven in extent, crossed by several highways and supporting Llys Helig and Castle Tremlydd, was obliterated by the action of the waves.

The destruction had been prophesied to Helig by a phantom voice heard whilst he was riding one evening. "*Dial a ddew! Dial a ddew!*" ("*Vengeance is coming! Vengeance is coming!*") said the voice. When Helig had recovered from the shock, he asked the invisible soothsayer "*When?*". He was relieved to receive the reply "*In the time of thy grandchildren, great grandchildren and their children.*" Not thinking any more of the prophecy, he returned to Llys Helig. Some time later, at a great feast, his family down to the fifth generation were celebrating at Helig's palace. Entering the cellar for more drink, a servant was horrified to find that water was seeping in. He only had time to warn the harpist of the danger, when suddenly a terrified cry of "*Tide!*" was heard, and a massive wave surged over Llys Helig, sweeping away the revellers.

It appears, however, that not everyone of Helig's entourage perished in the disaster, for in his *Essay on Welsh Saints*, Rice Rees wrote that "*While Helig was still living, his sons, upon the loss of their patrimony, embraced a monastic life in the colleges of Bangor Deiniol and Bangor Enlli.*"

The story of the sons of the profligate lord punished by divine wrath becoming converted and doing the Lord's work has already been mentioned in connection with the drunkard Seithenyn's destruction of Cantref y Gwaelod. A similar story of divine retribution by flood, echoing the exploits of the Biblical Noah, exists in Brittany in the legend of Caer Ys.

Helig ap Glannawg was actually the father of three docu mented Welsh saints; Boda, Gwynin and Brothen, recorded in the Penarth Manuscript and the Hafod Manuscript. St Gwynin and his brothers are supposed to have become monks at Bangor Fawr in Maelor. Later, some of his brothers (for tradition ascribes twelve sons to Helig), travelled through Wales, ending up at the monastery of Cor Cadfan in Bardsey. According to the old Welsh chronologies which record their exploits they lived "*at the time of Rhun ap Maelgwn*", about the middle of the sixth century.

Like Cantref y Gwaelod and Caer Arianrhod, Llys Helig and the Lavan Sands in general have attracted the attentions of antiquarian researchers. Intrigued by local tales of lost habitations, visitors have made plans and maps showing their reconstructions of Llys Helig, the ancient roads and the probable extent of the former coastline. In 1816, Edward Pugh wrote in Cambna Depicta: "*It is said that at very low ebb, ruined houses are seen, and a causeway pointing from Priestholm Island to Penmaenmawr*".

On the bottom of Conwy Bay there are remains which some have seen at low tide. They are traditionally ascribed to the remains of Helig ap Glannawg's palace, Llys Helig, and as such have been the focus of attention. They were visited in 1864 by Charlton R. Hall of Liverpool and the Reverend Richard Parry (better known as the Bard Gwalchmai) - of Llandudno. Hall noticed seaweed growing on erect structures which he believed to be the walls of the former palace. Later he wrote that he had seen the ruins of "*a grand old hall of magnificent dimensions, of whose shape and properties there still remain distinguishable traces.*" Hall also published a measured plan of Llys Helig.

In September 1908, W.Ashton visited the site and also found the remains of ancient walls. Horace Lees verified Ashton's discoveries in a visit of 1913, yet in 1939 when the archaeologist F.J. North saw the same site, he dismissed the stones there as merely natural, ignoring the million and a half tides which have scoured the site since its inundation. Ashton, however, had given a detailed description which can hardly be dismissed as fantasy.

"Three sides of a large square, with a large rectangular recess at the south west side, were seen to be well-defined by straight and almost continuous lines of wall, for the most part covered by a tall ribbon-like seaweed... these stones did not vary six inches from the straight line. There were two specially large stones, standing some 70 yards from the eastern corner, as if they had formed two pillars of a gateway... It is quite impossible for anyone to view these 350 or more yards of strictly rectangular remains and to entertain the slightest doubt as to their having been human handiwork."

Fragments of old buildings had been turning up for many years around the coast of North Wales and Anglesey. In *The History of Beaumaris*, published in 1669, William Williams wrote: "*wrought and carved free stones... have been found there... antient people of Ty Maur...had seen Iron barrs of Winders and other Irons come up from thence...*" Sir John Wynn of Gwydir, in a tract written between 1621 and 1626 (the year of his death), said of Llys Helig "*the Ruines whereof is nowe to bee seene uppon a Ground Ebbe some two Myles within the Sea directly over against Trevyn yr Wylva... unto which Hyll Helyg ap Glannog and his People did runn upp to save themselves, being endaungered with the sudden breakynge in of the sea uppon them, and there saved their Lyves.*"

According to Wynn, Helig had another manor, still visible in his day, at Pullhelo (Pwllheli), the present town being named after him. One very important remnant of the lands of Helig ap Glannawg is Priestholm, whose Welsh name is Ynys Seiriol or Puffin Island. Its original name was Ynys Lannog, named after Glannawg ap Helig Foel, father of the celebrated Helig. The name Priestholm, originally coined by Norse invaders, comes

26. The Pwllheli - Llanbedrog tramway was the last horsedrawn tramline in Wales. Here, then passengers are on their way to an eisteddfod in rainy weather in 1925, two years before the tramway was washed away by the sea.

from its association with Welsh monastic life, for Giraldus Cambrensis refers to it as Enis Lannach or *"the Ecclesiastical Island because many bodies of saints are deposited there, and no woman is suffered to enter it."* Priestholm, according to the Welsh chronicler, was *"inhabited by hermits, living by manual labour, and serving God."*

Before the irruption of the sea, Priestholm was an integral part of North Wales. Like the other largely lost monastic island of Hilbre off the Wirral peninsula of Cheshire, it afforded a relatively secluded place for the monks to build up psychic energies unhindered by the intervention of the profane. The foundation of the monastery is ascribed to St Seiriol, son of Owain Danwyn ap Einion Yrth ap Cunedda Wledig, traditionally known in Anglesey as Seiriol Wyn "the fair". *"From Priestholm to Penmen Mawr did Seirial cause a Pavement to bee made,"* wrote Sir John Wynn, *"Whereuppon hee might walk dry from his Church att Priestholme to his Chappel at Penmen Mawre, the Vale beynge very lowe Ground and wette... which Pavemt. may att this Day bee discerned from Penmen Mawre to Priestholme when the See is cleere, yf a Man liste to goe in a Bote to see ytt. Sythence this great and lamentable Innundacion, the Waye and Passage beyng stopped in this Straight in regard the Sea was come in... Seirial, lieke a good Heremite, did cause a Way to bee beaten and cutte through the mayne Rocke, which is the only Passage that is to passe that Straight."*

This causeway, which some believe to be the remains of a Roman road constructed when the area was dry land, is re corded by John Ray, whose 1662 Itinerary was published as Select Remains in 1760. In it he mentions a *"large paved Causey, visible at low water."* Ynys Seiriol, or Priestholm, was situated at the county boundary, whose delimiter was the now-lost River Ell, still mentioned in local legends and recorded in sixth century Arthurian romances. It is now completely beneath the waves.

All along the north coast of Wales are indications of former lands. In 1802, the following Welsh inscription was still visible in the churchyard wall at Abergele, between Rhyl and Colwyn Bay:

Ymamae ngorwedd,Y Monwent Mihangel Gwroedda iannedd dair milltir y gogledd Which translated into English, reads: "*Here lies, in the churchyard of St Michael's, a man whose dwelling was three miles to the northward.*" The churchyard is now less than a mile south of the present shore-line.

A quarter of a mile offshore in Colwyn Bay is Maen Rhys, named after a mythical shepherd called Rhys who, according to local folklore, used to sit upon it to watch his flocks grazing in the meadows that are now beneath the sea. Maen Rhys is also traditionally the site of a former castle. At Abergele, where the famous churchyard monument could once be seen, is a sandbank known as Constable's Bank, which was once land. Near St Tudno's church is a double row of upright stones leading northwards from a stone enclosure called Lletty Fadog to the edge of the cliff. This ancient British trackway was known as Hwlfa Ceirw, 'The Roadway of the Deer', because in former times it had provided access for animals and people across a high ridge to the lower lying pastureland by the sea shore. Truncated track ways like Hwlfa Ceirw are often indicators of lost lands.

Roads such as this would have been used by the defeated army of Brocmail in retreat from Chester after its rout by Ethelfrith, King of Northumbria, in the year 606. In one of the earliest pieces of documentary evidence of the north Wales lost lands, we read that the Welsh were forced to flee along the old Roman roads leading towards Anglesey. It is recounted that the Saxons followed the Welsh as far as Priestholm, now inaccessible except by boat. In 629, Cadwallon, a later Welsh ruler, was also blockaded there by the Northumbrian army under King Edwin. Access from there to Anglesey was across a relatively easy estuary, for in those days the formidable Menai Straits did not exist in their present form. Accounts of the Roman attack on the Druids in Anglesey tell of soldiers fording the strait, something that cannot be done today.

The island of Anglesey naturally has not been immune from the attacks of the sea that have devastated nearby coasts. Most of Newborough parish on the island had been swallowed up before the nineteenth century, and the Reverend W. Buckley, who travelled in Wales between 1798 and 1801 reported that he was prevented from reaching Holyhead by the bursting of a bank at Aberffraw which caused several hundred acres to be flooded at high water. Aberffraw was once the main royal town of Anglesey, northwest of which are the Maldraeth Sands, traditionally another lost land. Evidence for this is found at low tide. In *Mona Antiqua*, published in 1823, Rowlands said that he had seen there the ruined walls of houses and fields. These were detailed and listed as antiquities in the 1855 *Archzologia Cambrensis*. In the sands and shallows between Holyhead Island and Anglesey were also to be seen the remains of prehistoric cairns, marked as such on the earliest editions of the Ordnance Survey maps.

The names of the Welsh lost towns are instructive of the sort of situations they formerly occupied. Llys Helig, as well as echoing the name of its owner, can be translated as *"The Place of the Willow"*, occupying the junction of the rivers Conwy and Ell, the name of the latter meaning *"Eel River"*. Perhaps in antiquity the site was wooded and rural, rather than a tidal sandbank. Caer Arianrhod can be interpreted as the *"Town of the Silver Circle"*, appropriate in its connection with the Mother Goddess, who traditionally is connected with the moon. It must also be noted that the tides which destroyed the caer are con trolled by lunar gravitation. Caer Arianrhod was close to Bryn Aryn, the Silver Hill, whose corresponding solar counterpart, Bryn Eurian, the Golden Hill, marked the northern limit of Helig's land to the north.

Erosion on the coast of north Wales and Cheshire has been continuous: in about the reign of Edward III, the lands of Gronant were lost to the sea from the see of St Asaph's, and on the Meols shore of the Wirrall the dwellings were overcome by the sea and submerged beneath the waters of a permanent lagoon. Until the 1870s, the coastal marshes of Mostyn and Flint were pastures, but inroads of the sea reduced them to tidal mudflats. The Welsh port of Portmadog was saved from total destruction during the last century when a large causeway was constructed with great difficulty across the tidal flats in front of the town. The embankment was successful and is still used by the trains of the narrow gauge Ffestiniog Railway. One little-known result of Welsh coastal erosion was the closure of the last horse-drawn tramway on the British mainland; although horse trams still operate at Douglas on the Isle of Man. This archaic tramline ran along the shore of Tremadoc Bay between Pwllheli station and Llanbedrog, and by 1927 had become a tourist attraction in its own right. During the night of Friday 28 October that year, sudden and catastrophic seas destroyed the coast road and with it the tram track, and the line ceased operation.

The Wirrall Peninsula in Cheshire has long been the site of serious coastal depredations. Four of the most ancient roads and tracks there lead straight into the sea, and, like those in parts of Wales, Sussex and Norfolk, indicate the presence of former human habitation on land that no longer exists. Lying between the present estuaries of the Rivers Dee and Mersey, the Wirrall, now separate from Wales was formerly integral with it. The course of the River Dee once merged with the Mersey to the south of Liverpool, and the coastline was considerably different from that we know today. The testimony of local tradition, ancient maps and geological observation tells us that a serious and irrevocable change has befallen the area in relatively recent times. This lost territory, which went under the name of Leasowe, extended to the west and north-west of the present peninsula upon which Birkenhead now stands. In earlier times the land here was heavily afforested, as attested by the name of Birkenhead, which evokes the birchen wood still to be seen as tree stumps on the foreshore at Spring Tide. A memory of this forest survives in an old Cheshire rhyme.

Hilbre was an integral part of the land of Leasowe, later reduced to an island which has all but dwindled away. This 'birchen wood', of which Birkenhead is an unlikely reminder, was destroyed at an earlier date, some say during a cataclysmic incursion of the sea. William Webb, whose description of the Wirrall, written about 1615, was published in King's *Vale Royal*, commented on the remains of this forest in the "*mosses and turves*" (bogs) at Dove, thus: "*In these Mosses, especially on the*

Block, are Fir-Trees found under the Ground (a Thing marvellous!) in some places Six Feet deep or more. In others not One Foot; which Trees are of a surprising Length and Straight, having certain small Branches like Boughs, and Roots and one End as if they had been blown down by Winds; ... Some are of Opinion that they have lain there ever since Noah's Flood."

A poem of the same era refers to the trees *"at a place called Ye Stocks in Worold"*:

> *"But greater Woder calls me hence: Ye Deepe*
> *Low spongie Mosses yet remembrance keepe*
> *Of Noah's Flood: on Mumbers infinite*
> *Of Fir-Trees Swaines doe in their Casses light*
> *And in Summer Places, when Ye Sea doth bate*
> *Down from Ye Shoare, 'tis Wonder to relate*
> *How may Thousands of their trees now stand*
> *Black broken on their Rootes, which once drie Lande*
> *Did cover, whence Turfs Neptune yields to showe*
> *He did not Always to these Borders flowe."*

Exactly when these trees were laid low by the tide's catastrophic incursion is not known, but there is evidence that a serious and widespread subsidence took place in the area at some time after the Roman era. When the Ship Canal was being built, an ancient paved road was uncovered at Eastham, eighteen feet below the present ground surface, well below high tide levels. In the *Chester Archaeological Society Proceedings* for 1850, the Reverend Charles Massey reported that during the construction of the Chester Railway to Birkenhead Dock in 1845, the engineer, Mr Snow, discovered some remarkable remains. They consisted of four lines of oak bearing-beams carrying three equally-spaced horizontal spans. These were in turn found to be connected to abutments cut in the living bedrock. There were also the remains of rough stone piers. Massey concluded that here was an ancient Roman bridge in situ. The total length of this unique relic was over one hundred feet below that of the mean high tide mark.

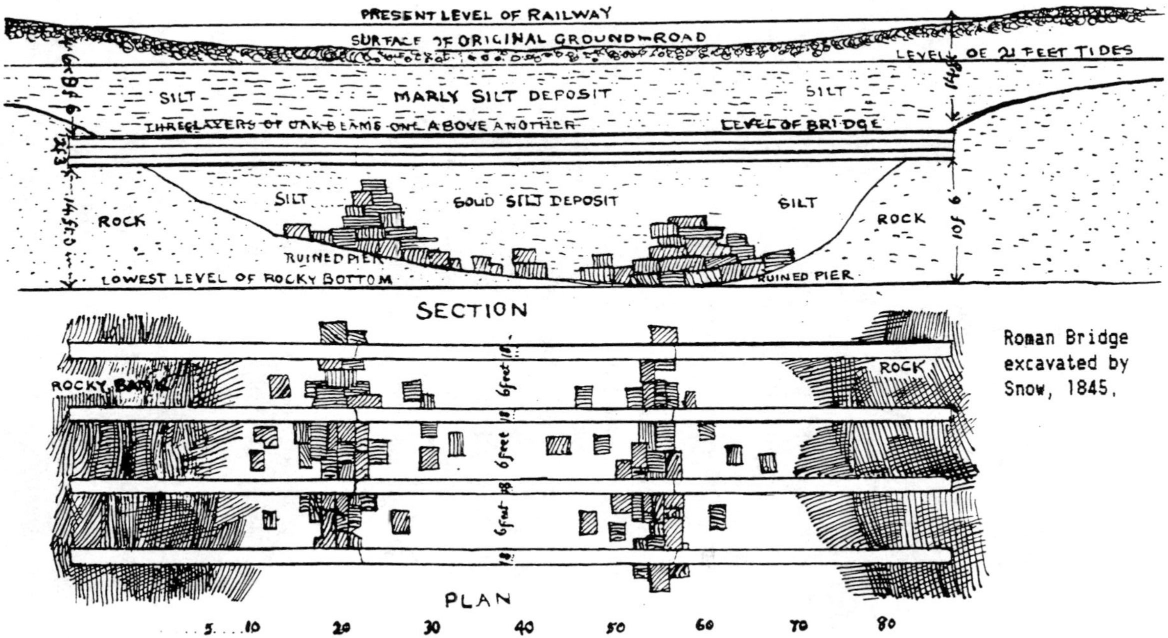

27. A plan and section of the Roman bridge excavated by Mr Snow, engineer-in-charge of the Chester Railway during the construction of its extension to Birkenhead in 1845.

Another piece of evidence supporting the subsidence theory was found during the construction of the gasworks at Chester about the same time. There, the remains of a Roman wharf were unearthed, being "*a kind of pier supported on oak piles, shod with iron set in concrete*". The tops of these piles, which would have originally supported wooden decking, were 20 feet below mean sea level. It must be noted that the subsidence required to bring the bridge and wharf to the depth at which they were discovered would account not only for the dissection of the once great Isle of Scilly into its present constituent archipelago, but also for the submersion of Cantref y Gwaelod, Caer Arianrhod, Llys Helig, the Mersey ford at Wallasey and, of course, Lyonesse. This incursion, or perhaps several incursions, were responsible for the wholesale sinking of various artifacts like Sarn Badrig and the Roman bridge, which would have been broken up and washed away if taken gradually by the forces of erosion.

One of these subsidence incursions doubtless destroyed the villages on the Meols shore of the Wirrall, where curious medieval remains were once found on the shore after an unusual tide. "*In 1890, traces of wheels of carts, horses' feet with round shoes, and the footsteps of cattle and of men who wore pointed shoes*" wrote Edward W. Cox, who visited the site, "*were for a short time visible on the ground below the level of high tide... by the side of the road were refuse heaps, containing bones, shellfish, fragments of iron, coal, cloth, and shoes similar to the footmarks.*" These remarkable relics were none other than the remains of the Meols villages submerged in a lagoon during a catastrophe in about the year 1400. Soon after Cox's visit, which must count as one of the first examples of 'rescue archaeology', the remains were swept away by fresh tides, and now nothing remains.

Tidal incursions caused great havoc in the Merseyside n region during the thirteenth century. In two great inundations the meadows of Stanlaw Abbey were destroyed, 150 acres being lost, and in 1296 the road between Ince and Stanlaw was obliterated. An extensive race-course formerly existed in Leasowe, but by 1600 it was '*decayed by the sea*'. The greater part of it succumbed to the sea during the nineteenth century. An ancient mansion, the manor house of Leasowe, fertile lands, public roads and burial grounds have all succumbed to the ocean. During surveys for a ship canal projected to connect the Mersey with the Dee, one of the engineers, Dr Nimmo, uncovered a number of human skeletons nearly opposite the Leasowe Lighthouse, about 200 yards seaward of the high tide mark. The skeletons were many in number and oriented correctly, showing them to be Christian burials, which led to the inescapable conclusion that here was the remains of a churchyard. The location of these inhumations was a shore-line as recently as 1771; gradual subsidence rather than erosion having lowered the graveyard wholesale beneath the waves.

At the turn of this century, an ancient holy well producing fresh water was still visible at low tide, and the remains of a brick arch that formerly covered it was still in evidence. it no longer exists. Tradition asserted that the last use of the well was to service a lighthouse, which, like many other buildings on that coast, has now been utterly extirpated. Erosion during the latter part of the eighteenth and the early part of the nineteenth centuries was so severe that in 1829 the Corporation of Liverpool built a sea-wall at Leasowe at the then great cost of £20,000. Extending from Leasowe Castle for two miles in a south-westerly direction, the sea defence effectively prevented the flooding of 3,000 acres of the Wirrall Peninsula.

The rate of erosion can be gauged from the fact that during the seventeenth century, Leasowe Castle was a full mile and a half from the sea. By 1850, the sea had encroached a mile nearer the walls and by the end of the nineteenth century it had been found necessary to build a masonry embankment to prevent the waves from demolishing the castle. The seriousness of the Wirrall erosion can be seen from the loss of 60 feet during a single storm on January 20th, 1863. Mr. Rollett, then the surveyor in charge of the Leasowe defences, estimated the annual loss to average out at an astonishing 18 feet. The erosive force of the estuarine waters of the Dee and Wirrall have long stirred the imagination of writers. In his Polyolbion, Drayton lyricized on the future fate of the Wirrall Peninsula thus:

> "Where Mersey, for more state,
> Assuming broader banks, himself so proudly bears,
> That at his stern approach extended Wirrall fears
> That what betwixt his floods of Mersey and of Dee
> In very little time devoured he might be."

The Rivers Dee and Mersey formerly communicated by a channel running to the south of the present Wirrall district. This channel has since become silted and reclaimed as farmland, but at the Dee's mouth, the old medieval town of Shotwick was washed away by the sea, only its massively-built church surviving into latter days. "*Whoever will survey that part of the Irish Sea now called the Liverpool Channel*", wrote a correspondent to *The Gentleman's Magazine* in July 1 796,"...*will not find it difficult to suppose, from the violence of the north-west sea upon this regular and pent-up situation that what now forms the banks of Burbo and Hoyle may have been land attached to the peninsula of Cheshire, and the eastern banks attached in like manner to Crosby and Formby, with the River Mersey running quietly through them, in a narrow inconsiderable stream, until such time as the sea, having once gained an accidental advantage, must have laid the foundation for that large expanse of water before and above the town of Liverpool which, though bearing the name of a river, is in reality a portion of the sea.*"

This assertion was borne out in 1828, when *The Liverpool Courier* announced that the bar from Rock Point to Wallasey Hole in the Mersey had been laid bare by the tide and had revealed the remains of an artificial ford composed of a number of stones between three and four feet in thickness. The Mersey was certainly a far more insignificant barrier than at present, for its crossing now precludes the use of a ford or even a bridge and is left to the tunnels for road and rail traffic.

The Dee, too, formerly presented less of a barrier. *The Gentleman's Magazine* correspondent asserted: "T*he like, it is probable, happened to the Dee; for, if we go a very few miles only up either of these apparently great rivers, we shall not find streams that shall satisfactorily of themselves account for such* *bodies of water."* At the present mouth of the Dee is Hilbre Island, formerly integral with Leasowe, a small remnant of an important monastic sanctuary. As late as 1575, Hilbre was still joined to the mainland for Llwyd's map of that year shows it so. The old Cheshire folk-poem cited above also records Hilbre's unity with the Wirrall.

Hilbre gets its name from the patron saint of a monastery that formerly existed there - St Hildeburgh's. Like the monastery on another piece of land that became an island - Priestholm Hilbre was sacred land, with the usual misogynist prohibitions of sanctuary. The monastic settlement dated from the Saxon period, when a large sandstone cross was erected there. Rediscovered during the nineteenth century, the cross was taken away by a local antiquary, Dr Hume, who considered it to be the same cross illustrated on Camden's map of the area. Traditionally, the cross marked the sacred omphalos of the area sacred to St Hildeburgh. The fragment removed by Hume was 23 inches across, but like so many antiquities removed from their original locations, it has subsequently disappeared from public view.

According to Drayton, Hilbre was known as the *"Corner of Wirrall"*. It is associated with one of those miracle stories so common in the 'lives' of the saints, assembled by monkish chroniclers during the middle ages. According to the story, in about the year 1120, Richard, the second Norman Earl of Chester, was threatened with rebellion at Basingwerk Abbey, near Holywell in Flintshire. Having received a courier's request for reinforcements, the Constable of Chester set out with his militia to find a ship to carry the reinforcements to Richard's aid.

The Life of St Werburge recounts that the Constable could find no ship to get him and his men across the Dee, but instead, a monk from St Hildeburgh's Monastery invoked the powers of St Werburge and caused a new sandbank to miraculously appear in the river, allowing the army to cross dryshod. The new pathway was known in later years as Constable's Sands.

Hilbre was strategically important, as the geomants who selected the monastery's site in Saxon times had recognised. Every ship entering or leaving the then major seaport of Chester, the old Roman city of Deva, was visible, whether the ship was sailing on an east wind by Chester Bar along the Welsh coast or a westerly through the Hoyle Lane and the Horse Channel. This strategic value was fully exploited during the Irish Rebellion of 1600, when the island became a transhipment point for the troops used in the suppression of the rebels.

In his *Memoirs of the Tyrone Rebellion*, Sir Henry Dockwra wrote: "*The Army, consisting in List of Four Thousand Foote and Two Hundred Horse, whereof Three Thousand of the Foot and all the Horse were levied in England... was Shipt at Helbre on the 24th of Aprille, 1600.*" Evidently, at that time, the now tiny island was large enough to station a large detachment of troops, being eight miles along by three broad. Leaving Merseyside, we come now to the coast of Lancashire, where erosion has added a further list of strange sounding names to the roll-call of lost towns. Just as the absence of megalithic remains near the coastline of the Cantref Y Gwaelod attest to lost lands, so a similar absence has been observed in south-west Lancashire. All along the coast are local tales of inundations, and the still-remembered names of Old Fornebei, Ravens Meols and Kilgrimod attest to the veracity of the legends.

In what is now Morecambe Bay were once the towns of Lowscales and Aldingham, whilst at the northern and southern end respectively of the Fylde coast were Singleton Thorpe and Waddon Thorpe. The Reverend W. Thornber's *Historical and Descriptive Account of Blackpool1*, published in 1837, gives a record of lands and villages submerged within historic times. According to Thornber, in 1554, during the reign of Mary 1, a sudden irruption of the sea took place at Rossall Grange, when a whole valley containing the village of Singleton Thorpe was swept away. Refugees from this disaster set up their tents further inland and thus founded a new village called Singleton.

To the south of Blackpool, the village of Waddon Thorpe existed on land now known as the Horse Bank, an offshore sandbank. "*In Furness also,*" wrote Thornber, "*a great part of the parish of Aldingham has disappeared; its church, formerly stand ing in the centre of the parish, is at present within high- water mark, and secured from the ravages of the sea by strong defences of mossy stone. The ruins of the village of Low Scoles were, within the memory of man, visible on the sands, and the hamlets of Crinleton and Ross are only known in records... a particular Sunday, about seventy-two to seventy-three years ago* [ie. 1764 or 1765 - NP.], *is named, when, owing to a change of current, caused by the bursting of some sandbank, or an elevation of the bottom of the sea, an immense body of water advanced to the shore at the influx of the tide. From that day our fathers date the recommencement of the encroachments on the land.*" Although the last century of Blackpool has firmly estab lished it as one of England's premier seaside resorts, local tradition still asserts that formerly the shore there extended much further out into the Irish Sea. Before Blackpool was founded, the village of Kilgrimod was on the coast, only to succumb to the tide. It is the site of yet another legend of bells tolling beneath the waves.

Scotland

The coastline of Scotland has always been more thinly populated with towns than its southern neighbour, and so the number of recorded lost towns is correspondingly much smaller. However, there are some notable losses. In Invernesshire, the town of Fort George and the surrounding coastal area have suffered considerable destruction, and in Morayshire the town of Old Findhorn suffered the fate of Dunwich and Ravenser Odd and was completely swept away. These losses were completely natural and unavoidable, but the village of Mathers, two miles to the south of Johnshaven in Kincardineshire was lost by human stupidity. Built on an ancient stable bank of shingle, the town was protected by the sea until quarrying for lime began there. So much lime was taken away by the workmen that the sea began to break through and in 1795 a massive storm swept away the whole village in a single night. The new coastline formed in that

28. *The remains of the Tay Bridge, December 1879.*

29. *Searching for the sunken train, Firth of Tay, December 30, 1879.*

night was 150 yards inland of the previous shoreline, and the regretful survivors were forced to build a new village further inland.

During the eighteenth century a considerable portion of the town of Arbroath was carried away by the sea, and the erosion at nearby Button Ness forced the removal of the lighthouses at the mouth of the Tay estuary, the foul weather of which was amply demonstrated in 1879 when the celebrated Tay Bridge went down in a gale, dragging with it a passenger train. At Button Point, the sea had advanced over three quarters of a mile in less than a century, so the designers of the Tay Bridge should have taken notice.

Elsewhere in Scotland, at St. Andrews, the Priory of Crail was undermined and swallowed up by the sea, and a tract of land at Cardinal Beaton between the castle and the shore was overwhelmed. In general, however, Scotland seems to lack those major towns and ports lost around the coasts of England and Wales.

North East England

Although there has been considerable land loss all along the east coast of England, the Holderness coast of Yorkshire has suffered more than most, and is perhaps the best documented. Further north, however, there are some formerly populous and important towns that have suffered obliteration. In County Durham, now Cleveland, the town of Seaton was formerly an important port, yet little now remains save a few relics noted at low tide. Nothing remains to the landward except the legend that an old chapel's ruins now lie beneath the local Golf Course. This may be the recorded chapel of St Thomas a Becket at Seaton.

Two miles south of the town was another, smaller town called Seaton Snook, but even less is known of this than its more northerly namesake. As late as 1667 a fortification was constructed there at the mouth of the river, but this, too, has vanished, though there have been the usual accounts of

30. Part of John Cary's map of the East Riding of Yorkshire with the Ainsty Liberty, London, c. 1811, showing Hartburn and Hyde, washed away by the German Ocean.

submarine forests being seen from time to time along this coast. Further south still between Bridlington and Skipsea was the erstwhile town of Hartburn, near to its twin town, Auburn.

The destruction of the east coast is nowhere more evident than at the curious place known to generations of seagoing men as Pennel's Pool. This anomalous area, now a considerable distance from the shore, is the site of the cliffs above which a notorious pirate of that name was hung on a gibbet as a reminder and a warning to mariners. Pennel's crime was the mutinous murder of his ship's captain, and the scuttling of the vessel off Hornsea. Taken prisoner, Pennel was tried and executed in London. His body was shipped back to the North in a crate marked 'glass'. The corpse was bound with iron hoops and, in 1770, was hung in a specially-constructed gibbet strategically placed on the North Cliff, visible for miles around. Neither gibbet nor cliff now remain, having long been claimed by the sea. That part of the coast has long suffered disastrous floods and erosion.

In the *Annals of Nicholas Trivet* we read of a catastrophic flood that took place on October 10th, 1253, when the Abbey of Meaux lost some of their estates at Myton, Saltaghe and Sutton. The flood completely destroyed the Abbey's possessions at Orwythfleet, and Tharlesthorp Grange was washed away. Holderness was notorious for coastal destruction, and the local inhabitants have fought a futile rearguard action against the sea throughout history. Erosion was so rapid that the Grange of Old or West Saltagh, constructed in 1160, had to be abandoned between 1197 and 1210 and reconstructed further inland.

Ancient maps show the extent of land losses. Saxton's map of Yorkshire published in 1577 shows a number of villages and towns that no longer grace the Holderness coast. He recorded Hornesie Becks, Sister Kirk, Kelseie Cliffe (Kilnsea), Pattentom Holmes (Patrington), Kennington, Pall, Hotton, Nothorpe, Pall, Dymiton, Out Newton and Hidon. Both Saxton in 1577 and Speed,1610 provided valuable cartographic records of the positions of towns and villages whose sole history often can be related as nothing more than that they once existed. In a map

31. A Forlorn remnant of Old Hartburn at the end of the nineteenth century, now washed away by the sea.

drawn in 1786 by J. Tuke, the towns of Hyde, Hornsea Beck, Hornsea Burton, Aldbrough, Old Withernsea and Frismarsh are shown as *"washed away by the sea"*.

The most important of the lost towns on this part of the coast was Hornsea, once a flourishing port with a pier and harbour, long since obliterated. As late as 1558, the pier existed, as evidenced by a 'Petition' of that year, but by the time of King James 1, it had been destroyed and the 2,500 tons of timber required to reconstruct it were not forthcoming. In 1609, an oath recorded: *"We find decayed, by the flowing of the Sea, since 1546, thirty-eight Houses, and as many Closes adjoining. Also we find two Churches since centuries far from the Sea. These were known, from the Similarity of their Architecture and from a Tradition which connected their Founders with close kinship, as Sister Churches."* One of these was the 'Sister Kirk' of Saxton. A tradition connected with the Hornsea church stated that the steeple bore an inscription that read: *"Hornsea Steeple, when I built Thee, Thou wast ten miles off Burlington, ten miles off Beverley, and ten miles off Sea."* Another local tradition asserts that Hornsea was originally thirteen miles from the sea.

Hornsea has also been the site of the discovery of a submarine forest, this one going by the name of Hornsea Wood. Like that at Owthorne, of which it was probably a continuation, Hornsea Wood has revealed the remains of animals. In 1836 a fine pair of antlers was discovered embedded in the remains of the forest at low spring tide. Along the coast, the old town of Hythe had vanished before the beginning of the fifteenth century. Burstall Priory, too, has left no traces save its name. This is the 'Burnstall Garth' shown on Saxtons invaluable map as three quarters of a mile south of Skeffling. Archaeological remains, however, are always being washed up along the beaches, the shore below Welwich having yielded many choice pieces, to the delight of generations of treasure-hunters and beachcombers. Saxon coins, the remains of a bronze fibula, a buckle of lead bearing the Lombardic letter A, and other attractive relics have been picked out of the black mud and sand thrown ashore from the deep after violent storms.

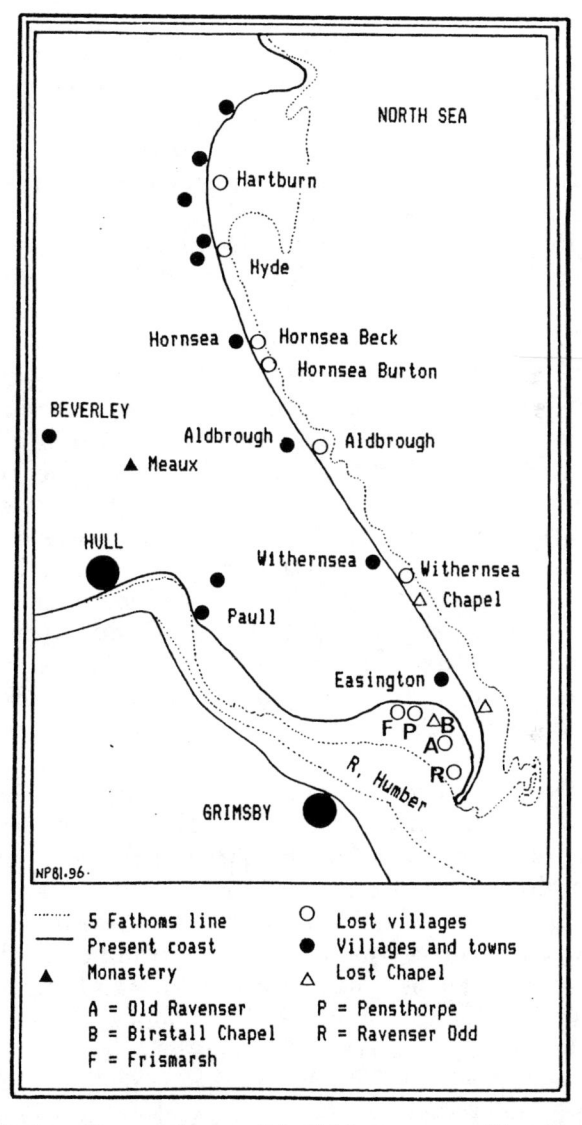

32. *Lost villages and towns of the Holderness coast of Yorkshire.*

It is easy to see how these fragments have ended up at the bottom of the sea, many details having been recorded of buildings going 'down the cliff' with their contents. At Owthorne, originally called Seathorne, the foundations of the churchyard were first undermined in 1786, so the church was then demolished before the sea could do the job. It was customary to deconsecrate and dismantle churches threatened with destruction, and instances exist all around the coast of this practice. The lost city of Dunwich, in Suffolk, is particularly notable on this account.

At Owthorne, during an unusually violent storm in 1816, the remains of the chancel went down the cliff into the sea, dragging with it many coffins and corpses in varying states of dissolution. After the storm, the vicar, the Reverend James Robson, inspected the remains at the foot of the cliff, and removed those bodies exposed by the sea but not washed away. One tomb broken open by the violence of the waves contained a rich burial. The person, generally acknowledged to have been the founder of the church, had been embalmed with aromatic spices which, even in 1816, had not lost their aroma. The corpse was swathed, Egyptian mummy-fashion, in bandages of seared cloth, and folded in a thin sheet of lead, which itself was painted. The corpse, along with several others, was removed to Rimswell churchyard where it was reinterred. Removal of the bodies to new place of sepulture was the only thing to do: by 1838 the churchyard at Owthorne had been utterly obliterated.

Six years later, the vicarage and other parts of the village followed the church down the cliff. The severe storms which caused such devastation to Owthorne in the early part of the nineteenth century also exposed most of the submarine forest. During the spring tide of December 1839, these fragments were exposed, and various types of tree were identified by the curious investigators, who also noted acorns, hazel and beach nuts, even the roots of reeds. Various animal bones were excavated, including a stag s antler 10.5 inches in length. The whole coastline suffered severely during that period, and at Hornsea and Withernsea, ships were driven right through the churches.

Old Withernsea was another important Holderness settlement. According to Poulson, the 'historian of Holderness', "The Old Township of Withernsea stood beyond that which is now the Cliff, and that the Row of old Enclosure called the Row Garths, were all that remained of the situation at the time of enclosure." Here, as on the coasts of Sussex, Norfolk and Wales, the ancient landscape patterns attest to a former town beyond the present coastline. Like other towns on the Holderness coast, Withernsea saw official government inspections during the Middle Ages. The siting of new churches was of course a solemn and important business, and special commissions of geomants often studied the area for long periods before deliberating on the correct site. On November 8th, 1444, such a geomantic com mission arrived at Withernsea to decide upon the site for a new church, the old one having just been wiped out in a storm.

Old Kilnsea, too, lasted only until the early part of the nineteenth century, when its church was destroyed. It is thought that the present Kilnsea may have been as much as a mile inland of the old town of the same name. Between the compilation of the Domesday Book in 1086 and 1900, about 1,275 acres of land of Kilnsea Parish were wiped out, over seventy per cent of the whole. The church lasted until 1823, not long after the doom of that at Owthorne. The final service was held as the church teetered on the edge of a crumbling cliff, and the church itself was demolished in 1826.

The village of Atwick is another gauge of the rapidity of Holderness erosion, for when it's cross was erected in the middle ages, it was more than two miles distant from the sea. By 1786 a survey revealed that the cross was only 33 chains and 611inks from the cliff, and by 1830, half as much again of that distance had gone.

Hartmut Valentin has provided us with the most recent calculation of the late of loss on the Holderness coast. In 1952 he carried out accurate measurements of the exact position of clifftops from nearby topographical features such as old houses, footpath junctions, hedges, ditches and other boundary markers.

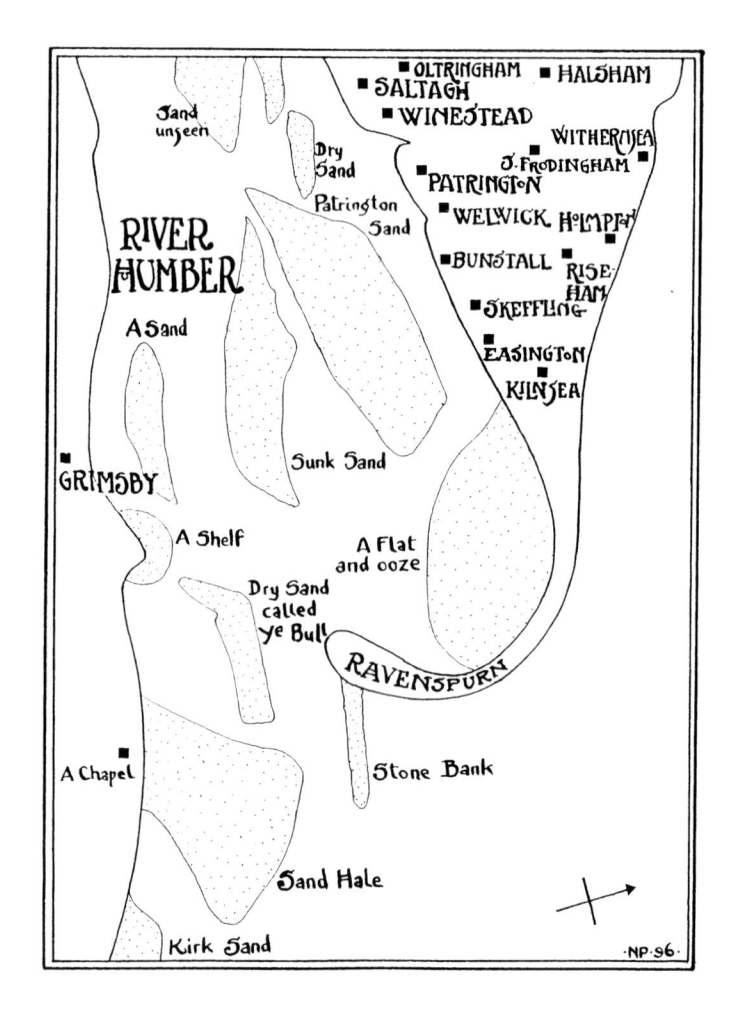

33. The mouth of the River Humber, after Lord Burleigh's Chart, c. 1580.

He then identified these reference points on the earliest 6-inch maps of the Ordnance Survey (1852 edition), and on account of the large scale he was able to determine cliff-top positions to within 10 feet. By comparing the 1852 map with the 1952 fieldwork, Valentin was able to calculate the erosion over a full century. He took altogether 307 measurements at intervals of about 200 yards along a 38 mile stretch of coastline and found that at almost every place there had been a land loss of between a few inches and five feet per annum. The approximate loss for the entire Holderness coast between Sewerby and Kilnsea Warren was annually 4 feet, totalling more than 760,000 square feet a year.

The place known to posterity as Old Ravenspur is unique in British history as being a lost land of vital importance in the history of the nation. Ravenspur was the landing-place of three royal aspirants and their retinues, the origin-point of three coups d'etat which overthrew the current monarch. The whole area, apart from the promontory of Spurn Head, is no more, having been obliterated by the tides and currents of the treacherous River Humber. Spurn Head was Spurenhead in Old English, from the Anglo-Saxon *Spyrian* or *Spyngean*, to look out, or to watch. Being an important land-mark as well as a hazard to shipping, the point has long been marked by a watch-tower or beacon. Camden wrote that "*on the very tip of the promontory, where it draws most to a point, and is called Spurnhead, stands the little village of Kellnsey*" which sported a watch-tower, hence the spy connotation.

From its shape, we can see that Spurn Head has been formed by the sea's currents, altering gradually over the years. In his book Lectures on Sewers, published in 1622, Collis wrote "*Of late Years Parcel of the Spurnhead, in Yorkshire, which before did adhere to the Continent, was torn therefrom by the sea, and is now in the Nature of an Island.*" Since then, it was reconnected to the mainland, but in 1995 it was again cut off. In the lee of this promontory is an area of sands still known as the Old Den (from the Anglo-Saxon *den*, a hole or hiding-place). The Old Den consists of a semicircular ridge of gravel half a mile long and about seventy yards wide, raised about a yard above the surrounding mudflats. The famous old town of Old or Ald Ravenser or Ravenspur existed in this Old Den, and as late as the turn of the eighteenth century, Humberside fishermen asserted that at low water there were to be seen there the remains of buildings.

The traditional site of Ravenser was investigated during the last century by William Child of Easington. According to his account, reported in Beccles Willson's The Story of Lost England, "*In digging on a place within the present Spurn Point, called the Old Den, we found Ashlar stone, chiselled and laid in lime; seemingly the foundation of some building of note; the heads of the piles also having been found.*" Ravenser was a town of some note and some antiquity. It is first mentioned in an eleventh century Icelandic poem by Stein Hardisson, *Olafs Drapa* (Olaf's Praise), in which it is called Hrafnseyrr. Etmologically, Hrafnseyrr means "*the point of Raven's promontory*", from *Hrafn*, raven, and *eyrre*, Old Norse for a promontory. The associated place-name of Ravenser Odd derives also from the Old Norse: *oddi* meaning a point of land, as in the last syllable of Kilgrimod, the lost Lancashire town off Blackpool. Tradition states that Ravenser was the place from which a small band of Norsemen, the straggling survivors of the disastrous Battle of Stamford Bridge in 1066 took final leave of these shores.

In about 1234, a small island was '*born of the sea*', as a Grimsby chronicler describes the event. Accretion of gravels, perhaps around the nucleus of a shipwreck, driven perhaps by a surge tide or some other abnormal tidal occurrence, had made a sand bank poke above the general level of the Humber estuary. Once formed, the island grew in size, and one day a ship ran aground on it and could not be refloated. The hulk remained there, abandoned, until it became the home of an enterprising tradesman who set himself up in business selling provisions to the crews of passing vessels. The Lord of Holderness, William de Fortibus, thought the island sufficiently lucrative to be taken over for his own profit, so he sent over a bailiff and some villeins to found a hamlet there on his behalf. it soon received the name

34. The Ravenser Cross in its latter-day location at Hedon.

of Ravenser Odd or Ravensrod, and, being further out in the channel than any other inhabited place with landing facilities, fishermen soon found it a convenient place to come ashore to dry their nets and to re-stock with provisions and other necessities of the seafaring life.

The new town grew and prospered, and King Henry iii granted the town the right to hold a weekly market and an annual fair lasting sixteen days, which proved another draw for shipowners. During this time, Old Ravenser was overshadowed and most of its inhabitants left for the new town, reducing it to little more than a manor house with its attendant outbuildings. The Monks of Meaux Abbey, always with an eye to a good business proposition, soon gained a piece of the action and obtained a share in the profits of Ravenser Odd. The earliest actual dated reference to Ravenser Odd's ownership come from this period, in 1251, when "Rowenserat" was held by the Lord of Holderness. In the *Chartulary of Meaux Abbey* is recorded the gift of half an acre of land at a place called the "Burg of Odd, near Ravenser", where the monks were given permission to erect buildings for the kippering of herrings and other fish for the use of the Abbey's inmates. The monks also set up the first church at Ravenser Odd, subordinate to the parish church at Easington.

Townsmen of Ravenser Odd were well placed to get rich. They took to "forestalling" ships bound for Grimsby, offering better prices for their fish, and generally taking trade away from the old-established port. In 1290, complaints to King Edward I brought Grimsby no redress, and insult was added to injury when both Kingston-upon-Hull and Revenser Odd, which had not long existed, were granted the privileged status of 'free port' on payment of £300 to the king. By the end of Edward l's reign Ravenser Odd was sending two burgesses to represent its interests in Parliament, but less than a century after the sandbank had first reared itself above the water, the town underwent a sharp decline.

All along the Humber, the unpredictable tides had been playing havoc with the coastline. At Orwythfleet, for example, 33 acres of grassland were carried away by the sea between the years 1310 and 1339. According to a letter addressed in 1301 by Abbot Corbridge to the Prior and Convent of Gisburn, in that year a funeral cortege was conveying a body from Hull chapel to Hessle for burial when a flood tide of the Humber washed everybody away. By the fourteenth century, travelling between Anlaby and Hull had become so hazardous that it became necessary to raise the road six feet above its former level.

Just as the island of Ravenser Odd had appeared without warning, its end was no less dramatic. In the days of Hugh of Leven, Abbot of Meaux (1339-49), the waves of the Humber almost destroyed the chapel and the greater part of the town, after which it was largely abandoned. During the time of the next Abbot, William of Drynghowe (1349-53), the chapel was entirely destroyed and the bodies buried in its graveyard were disinterred by the sea. The end of Ravenser Odd came in a terrifying manner. According to the *Meaux Chronicle*, the waves had *"risen above the town and surrounded the place like a solid wall"*. The few left flocked together and perambulated the town, with a priest carry ing the consecrated host and the townspeople the relics of saints, a cross and ecclesiastical ornaments, in a last-ditch attempt to invoke God's intervention. After this scare, the town was finally abandoned, and the refugees attempted to found a new town at Drypool. The authorities forbade this, and the refugees dis persed.

The state of the area at that time can be gauged from a 1346 confirmation made to the Chapter of York with regard to the appropriation of the church at Easington, made by William, Archbishop of York, to the Abbey of Meaux. The grant specified the manors of Salthagh, Tharlesthorpe, Frismersk, Wythefleet, Dymalton and Ravensrodd in Holderness as ancient endow ments of the Abbey, being greatly reduced by the depredations of the sea. *"From day to day"*, said the confirmation, *"these places become so far wasted, being tossed by impetuous waves every day and night, that within a very short time it may be feared that they will be altogether destroyed and consumed."*

Owing to this devastation, an Inquisition was taken at Ravenser Odd regarding the run-down state of the town and its inability to pay its taxes. The burgesses examined declared that *"two parts and more"* of the town's *"tenements and soil"* had been beaten down and carried away by the sea, and the *"the said town is daily diminished and carried away"*. Most of the inhabitants, seeing the hopeless situation, had already fled from the dwindling town, as *"the dangers there continue to increase from day to day... so that there does not remain a third part of the inhabitants with their goods, who are in any manner able to sustain the present charges and assessments."*

The town was officially abandoned, and the municipal authorities and rights suppressed. According to the *Torres Manuscript*, in 1355 a major storm devastated one of the principal burial grounds of Ravenser Odd, washing away many of the bodies. This sacrilegious state could not be tolerated by devout people, so the Abbot of Meaux was directed to gather up the remains and give them Christian burial in another parish. Another major inroad of the ocean occurred in 1377, and the remaining sandbank went beneath the waves, along with the villages of Frismarsh, Redmare, Pennyswerll, Potterfleet and Ipsal. All that remained was a causeway which formerly connected Ravenser Odd with the mainland, and by the end of the fourteenth century, Burton, compiler of the *Meaux Chronicle*, knew the place only as Odd-juxta-Ravenser, a mudbank.

Longer established and longer lasting than Ravenser Odd was the town of Old Ravenser, site of an important fair. The fair at Ravenser began *"on the Eve of the Nativity of Our Lady, continuing for thirty following days; for that time will be very profitable to the King; and also a market two days in every week, that is to say, on Tuesday and Saturday; and that may be free of tonnage."* Thus Ravenser was given virtual free port status.

Fairs of such duration were not uncommon in places strategically placed for trade; the famous Sturbridge Fair near Cambridge, immortalised by Daniel Defoe, continued for two months every year, for Cambridge was then an important port with access to the sea, and Ravenser was even better favoured. Long fairs like Sturbridge and Ravenser provided important meeting-places for businessmen, and even promoted the exchange of religious and political ideas in an era when travel was the exception rather than the norm.

Ravenser had two main streets interconnected with several subsidiary alleys and lanes, a number of churches, a gate at either end of the town and probably an establishment of the Knights Hospitaller. The fair granted to the town was one indication of its importance: another can be gauged from the fact that the Grace Dieu, the largest merchant vessel of the age, was built on the orders of John Taverner, son of Thomas Taverner, Member of Parliament for Old Ravenser.

Ravenser existed on the tract of land called 'Ravenspur' by several chroniclers, including William Shakespeare. This tract of land included the present Spurn Head, the town of Old Ravenser and the area at the mouth of the River Humber incorporating the land now reduced to mere sandbanks. Roughly triangular in shape, this tract of land was held in British esoteric tradition to be a key point in the overthrow of kings, and indeed three pretenders to the thrones of England or Scotland actually used the place as a landing-point.

In 1332, Edward Balliol, who had for several years been exiled in France, decided to lay claim to the crown of Scotland. Encouraged by the English king, Edward iii, Balliol prepared to seize the throne by force. Aided by the lords Beaumont, Mowbray and Wake, Balliol decided that the attack upon his homeland should be by sea, so he set out from Ravenspur with his army of 3,000 men-at-arms in ships obtained from the Humber ports. Balliol's attack was a success, for he gained for himself the crown of Scotland.

In 1399, Bolingbroke, Duke of Lancaster, afterwards King Henry IV, landed at or near the place used by Balliol to launch his armada against Scotland. This time, the crown at stake was that of England. In his play Richard Ii, William Shakespeare immortalised the act in the words he gave the Earl of Northumberland:

> *"Away with me in post to Ravensburg,*
> *But if you faint, as fearing to do so,*
> *Stay and be secret, and myself will go."*

Holinshed's Chronicle, Shakespeare's source, asserts that Bolingbroke landed there with threescore persons, and was joyfully received by the lords, gentlemen and knights of the country. *'The banished Bolingbroke repeals himself, And with uplifted arms is safe arriv'd At Ravenspurg"*, wrote Shakespeare.

When the Duke of Lancaster and his small party landed at Ravenspur in June 1399, he noticed workmen standing by the foundations of a new building. Curious as to the nature of the new structure, the future king enquired of Matthew Danthorpe, the monk supervising building operations, what was going on. The monk replied that he was erecting a chapel to be dedicated to the Virgin Mary on the site, but this did not please the Duke, for Royal approval had not been granted. A sacred place was being erected upon geomantically important ground without permission from the King - it had not been vetted and sanctioned by the King's advisers expert in the assessment of geomancy. However, the future King, having landed successfully, may have felt that the chapel's siting was beneficial, and permitted the monk to proceed with construction.

That this *"triangular place"* was held to be geomantically significant for the arrival of three claimants of the throne at Ravenspur seems to have been in fulfilment of a traditional prophecy. According to this prophecy, ascribed to the wizard Merlin, or alternatively to the Christian holy man Bede, the place was destined to be important in British history: *"There shall be a king in Albion"*, went the prophecy, *"who shall region for the space of twenty and two years in great honour and great power, and shall be allied and united with Gaul; which king shall be undone in the parts of the North in a triangular place."*

Although one tradition connects the saying with Merlin, it does not come from the version cited in Geoffrey of Monmouth's *History of the Kings of Britain*. In the era of Henry IV, prophecies and omens were held in great regard, and the utterances of soothsayers were taken with deadly seriousness. The prophecies of 'long-range' soothsayers like Merlin, Martha the Gipsy and Mother Shipton are but fragmentary remains of the vast literature of prophecy which formerly existed in England. Henry would certainly have been aware of the prophecy, and would have seen himself as a fulfilment of it.

In September 1399, Henry became King Henry IV upon the overthrow of Richard 11. On his seizure of the throne, Henry sent the humble hermit of Ravenspur a document authorising him to complete his hermitage and chapel and giving him full rights over the sands and seas for a radius of two leagues from the chapel's omphalos. "*Whereas Matthew Danthorpe, Hermit,*" read the authorisation, "*hath begun to build a new chapel in Ravenspurgh, at which on our last coming to England, we landed (our license not being obtained on this matter) ... the said Matthew may... proceed in the completion of the same chapel, of our superior grace, we have pardoned and remitted to the same Matthew all manner of transgressions and misprisions on his part committed, and whatsoever he hath forfeited to us, or whatever penalty he hath incurred on the aforesaid occasions. Witness the King at Westminster, this first of October, 1399.*"

Shortly afterwards, Danthorpe died and his post was taken over by Richard Reedbarrowe. Several years and two reigns later, Reedbarrowe wrote a petition to King Henry VI's parliament, describing the hazards of the Spurn Head, how "*oft-times, by misadventure, many divers vessels and men, goods and merchandise, be lost and perished, as well by day and night, for default of a beacon that teach the people how to hold in the right channel.*" He related how he had begun "*in the way of charity, in salvation of Christian people, to make a tower, to be upon daylight a ready beacon, and wherein shall be light given by night to all the vessels that come into the said River of Humber.*" But as construction work cost money, the hermit continued, "*the which tower may not be made nor brought to an end without great cost"* he told Parliament.

Parliament was impressed by such an obviously beneficial project, and authorised that the hermit should be permitted to levy a tax on all vessels coming into the port Hull so that the moneys raised could pay for the lighthouse and keep the light tended. So by 1427, a beacon stood on Spurn Head to save many a thankful mariner from shipwreck.

In 1428, Richard Reedbarrowe was described as *"the poor Hermit of the Chapel of Our Lady St Ann at Ravenserspurn"*. The possibility of an earlier lighthouse or watchtower there has already been noted in connection with the etymology of the place-name. The hermit's name, Reedbarrowe, also hints at more than meets the eye, for it has connotations of measurement and earthworks. Perhaps he was one in a long line of initiate guardians of the sacred site.

The landing of the future King Henry IV was not the last event in English history affected by Ravenspur, for in 1471 another claimant of the throne landed there. On the deposition of King Henry Vl in 1461, Edward IV was declared king, and the nation had descended into the bloody and barbarous civil war now euphemistically known as the Wars of the Roses. The oddly-favoured part of the country played its part in the temporary eclipse of the new king in 1469, when the Yorkists forced Edward to flee the country. After this setback, Edward resolved to regain the throne, and here the 'Ravenspur connection' comes in yet again to alter the history of the British monarchy. With 2,000 soldiers in eighteen ships, Edward landed *"within Humber, on Holdernesse side, at a place called Ravenspurgh, even the same place where Henry, after called King Henry IV, landed."* Edward's invasion, like Henry's, was successful, leading to the downfall of the restored King Henry Vl and his murder in prison.

Relics of the once-important triangular place are now few. The attrition of centuries and a general abandonment of the area to the elements has left Ravenspur to revert to nature. One ancient

35. Before the renewal of sea defences in the early 1990s, boards and sandbags were a common sight in the Norfolk town of King's Lynn at times when high tides threatened flooding.

monument was a cross that formerly stood at a place called Ravenscrosbourne, possibly erected to commemorate the landing of Henry of Lancaster, though probably earlier in date. The cross showed Christ wearing a short loin cloth, with his arms nearly straight, head erect without the crown of thorns, beardless and with legs not crossed but side by side and fixed with two nails instead of the traditional one. Stylistically, the cross may have been Norman or even pre-conquest like the famous Rood at Romsey Abbey. Known as the Ravenser Cross, it was moved at some time to Kilnsea, and when that place was undermined, to Burton Constable and finally, during the last century, by James Watson to Hedon. Heraldic devices on the cross have been traced to the arms of the Nevil family. Ralph Nevil, Earl of Westmoreland, was one of the supporters of Henry IV, and this

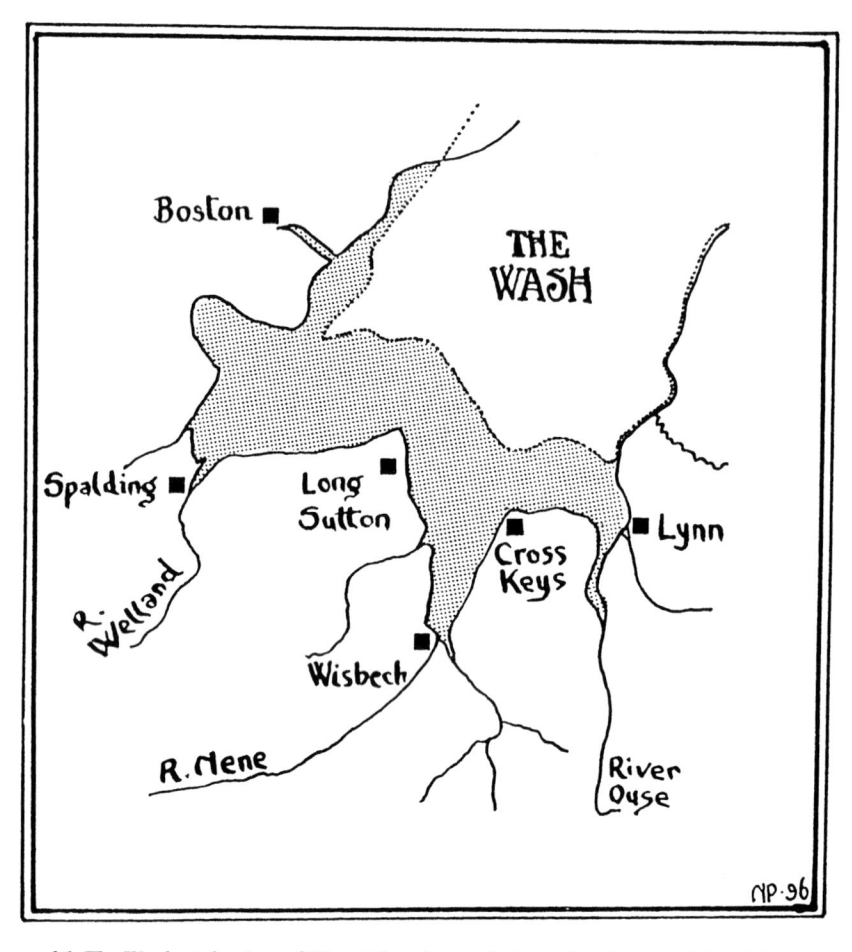

36. *The Wash at the time of King John: the shaded area has been reclaimed since the king lost his treasure whilst crossing a treacherous causeway. King John's treasure remains to be discovered!*

has been taken as concrete evidence that the cross was indeed commemorative of the Lancastrian landing of 1399. If so, it is another example of a geomantic structure erected to ensure a favourable future for the king.

Lost Lincolnshire and East Anglia

"Half-sunk in the sea, half-vanished from the eye of man, a great name in history, and a fading name in the present, the former capital of East Anglia is today an impressive and pathetic spectacle as its cluster of small cottages is viewed dipping down towards the ravenous ocean."
    Cuming Walters: *Bygone Suffolk* (1901)

Like the Cambridgeshire levels, the Lincolnshire Fens are the result of severe and prolonged flooding in antiquity. The remains of large trees, 'bog oaks', are still frequently discovered during digging and ploughing operations, evidence that the flat and largely treeless area of to-day was formerly flourishing woodland. Some of the trees excavated from the peat have been substantial. An oak found at Bardney was 90 feet long and four feet square, containing 1440 'feet' of solid timber. Such trees have been found at fen drainage; workmen laying a new sluice at the fall of Hammond Beck into Boston Haven encountered the roots of trees still embedded in the soil, showing that the former ground level was much lower, below high water mark of the tide. Dugdale relates that at the laying of Skynbeck Sluice near Boston they found the remains of a smithy complete with tools and horseshoes, sixteen feet below ground level.

The catastrophe which reduced flourishing woodland to wet fen seems to have been post-Roman in date, probably caused by a tidal wave of great dimensions. The early antiquaries Dugdale and Stukeley were of the opinion that the disaster was occasioned by an earthquake which lowered the level of the land by several feet. *"Granting, therefore, that this country, though lying flat and low, was not originally annoyed with the inundations of the ocean,"* wrote Dugdale, *"I am now to*

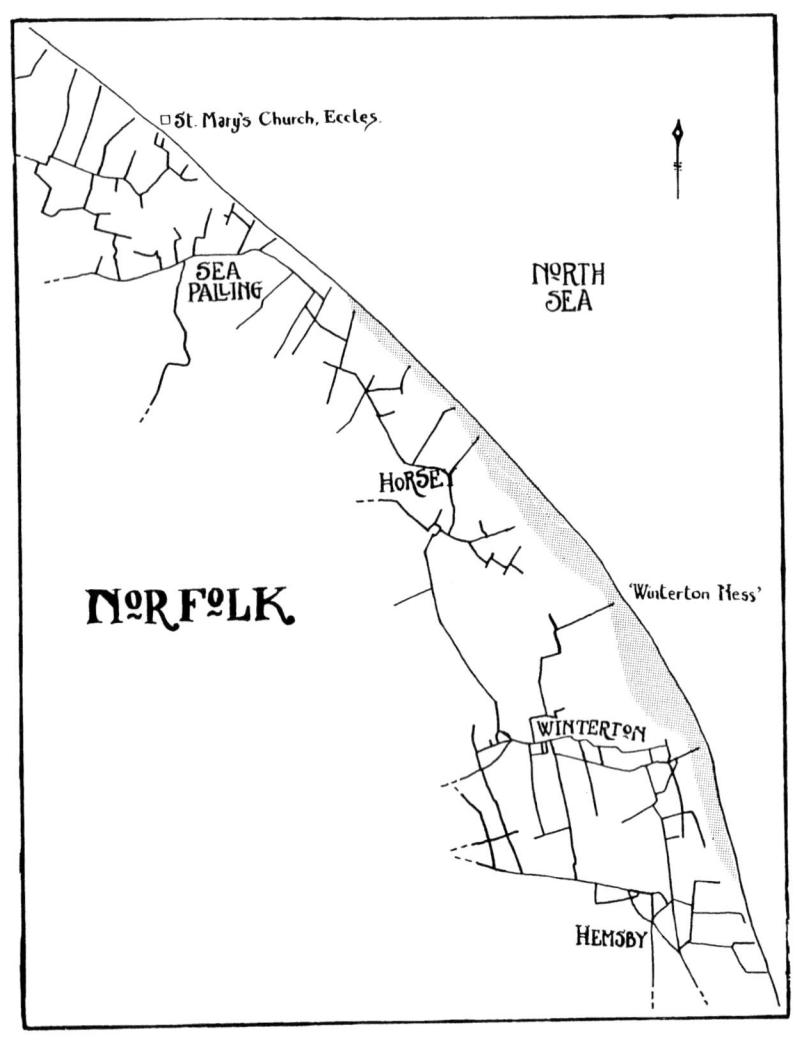

37. *The road pattern of east Norfolk is a remnant of a system that once extended much further east, where the North Sea now rules.*

38. *The west door of St Margaret's Church in Kings's Lynn bears the record of many floods, the highest on record of which was on January 11, 1978.*

demonstrate by what means it came to pass that the ocean broke into it with great violence, as that the woods then standing throughout the same became turned up by the roots; and so great a portion of silt brought in as did cover the ground in an extraordinary depth, even to the remotest parts on the verge of the highlands."

This silt, evidence of a major flood disaster, was noted by Mr Edwards in his 1769 Survey of the Witham, when he cited forest remains at Bodiam Sands near Bardney. *"They consist of a thin bed of sand upon a bed of strong blue clay,"* wrote Edwards, *"On which bed was found a large number of oak, yew and alder roots and trees, which had grown theron... the oak roots stand upon the sand, and tap-root into the clay; some of the trees are five feet in diameter at the bole, and more than ten feet from out to out at the root."* Although the dating of the flood is vexed with problems, it has been suggested that it took place in about the year 500, the likely date of the Lyonesse catastrophe and the loss of the Welsh lands. One fanciful theory attributes the name of the Saxon kingdom of Mercia to the overflowing of Lincolnshire and the Cambridgeshire Fens during the Heptarchy, as Henry of Huntingdon, writing in 1154, called it *"Fenny Country"*; there was obviously no written record or recent memory of such an inundation. Of lost towns, there is not a great amount recorded. Old Skegness was formerly a walled town with a castle and harbour, destroyed in the medieval period. *"Skegnesse was at sumtyme a great Haven Towne"* asserts Leland, *"The Old Towne is clene consumed and eten up with the Se. Part of a Chirche of it stode of late. For Old Skegnesse is now builded a poor new Thing."*

Cromer and Sheringham

To the north of Skegness, the areas around Trusthorpe, Sutton on Sea, Chapel St Leonards and Lincolnshire, Norfolk, too, have suffered severely from marine attrition. One important lost town was the former seaport of Shipden - spelt variously in *Domesday Book* as Shipedana, Scepedana, Scipidene and Scipedana. it

39. The eroded cliffs at Hunstanton, Norfolk, showing how the sea defences have prevented the cliff falls further east. The eroded cliffs are a notable nesting-place of Fulmars.

stood to the north of the present town of Cromer, of which the earliest documentary notice of coastal erosion dates from 1337, when the rector of Shippey juxta-Mare, John de Lodbrok, the patron of the church, John Brown, and the parishioners supplicated Edward iii for leave to construct a new church. Their old church, dedicated to St Peter, was threatened by the sea. Permission was granted, and the new church, called Shipden-juxta-Felbridge, was built at the site of the present Cromer church. Old St Peter's was swallowed up by the sea between 1338 and 1391. As late as 1937, Church Rocks, as the remains of Old Shipden church came to be called, were visible off Cromer at low spring tides.

As Shipden slowly succumbed to the waves, so Cromer grew and prospered. Shipden having finally been disposed of, the sea continued its advance, and in 1611 claimed the greater part of the Weylands Manor off Cromer. In the winter of 1799 half an acre of cliffs was washed away near the lighthouse, and on January 15th 1825, a 25-acre piece of land fell into the sea, over half a million cubic yards of earth and rock in a single day. Early in the morning of August 19th, 1832, another massive portion of cliff was washed away near the lighthouse. This fall threatened to undermine the beacon, so another was built 250 yards further inland to replace it. This proves to have been a sensible measure, for on the night of December 5th-6th 1866 the last remnants of the old lighthouse went down the cliff.

At Sheringham, west of Cromer, it was recorded that in 1829 the water was 20 feet deep where only 48 years earlier a 50 foot cliff had stood. Between the years 1805 and 1829 the cliffs receded over 60 feet at lower Sheringham. Trimingham was reduced from a large parish to a small village and in the 60 years preceding 1844, over 50 acres were lost. One tide is recorded as having taken away four and a half acres. Keswick is now no more than a name on the map at the cliff's edge just south of the North Sea Gas terminal at Bacton. Like Overstrand, it has disappeared into the sea. Just south of Happisburgh, the village of Whimpnell, too, is completely gone, being survived by a small cluster of houses called Whimpnell Green about a mile from the cliff edge.

Waxham and Little Waxham are also virtually gone, all that remains are a church and a hall standing amid the sand dunes.

Eccles

Eccles was once a hamlet of the Great Lordship of Happisburgh, and its parish consisted of over 2,000 acres of farmland. In 1605, during the reign of King James 1, the parishioners petitioned the king for a reduction in taxes because by then there were only 14 houses and 300 acres left. By 1844, the village had been completely engulfed and the parish reduced to a mere 150 acres. In 1839 the encroaching sea laid bare the foundations of dwellings, the chancel end of the church and a portion of the churchyard walls. After this, the village was abandoned, but the church tower survived on the beach as an attraction for sightseers and a landmark for mariners. On January 23rd 1895, the tower finally fell during a storm, but the rubble can still be seen today at low tide.

Eccles is on the part of the Norfolk coast that has suffered the worst coastal erosion. Between Winterton on-Sea and Weybourne, it is estimated that between two and three miles have been lost in the last 2,000 years, having completely destroyed the former promontory of Winterton Ness. The coast in the vicinity of Great Yarmouth, unlike that to the north and south, has not suffered severe erosion, but has been built up. In Roman times, the land now occupied by Great Yarmouth was an island, and the now-inland Burgh Castle where one of the Forts of the Saxon Shore still stands, was originally on the coast. During the early medieval period, Yarmouth be came joined to the mainland, and has been ever since.

The famed Scroby Island off Yarmouth, a sand bank that periodically becomes dry except at high tide, is at present undergoing destruction, like the coast of Gorleston-on-Sea a mile to the south. Coastal erosion over a mere eighty years has reduced the Gorleston beach to insignificance. "The village of Gorleston, a suburb of Yarmouth," wrote Cuming Walters in 1901, *"is now a thriving and rapidly-growing watering-place,*

40. The church tower on the beach at Eccles, which fell in 1895.

41. Fragments of Eccles Church can be found at low tide.

famous for its hard, wide sands, and its violent tides." Postcards still on sale there today show a wide beach seaward of the boating pool, but, at high tide, waves now pound on its walls. Since 1978, large rocks have been obtained and dumped on the beach in front of the sea wall, whilst the corporation has even had to resort to importing lorryloads of sand from elsewhere to prevent the beach from disappearing entirely. It is surely only a matter of a few years before the sea permanently assaults the sea wall.

Further south, the village of Newton once stood to the north of Lowestoft between Corton and the sea, but the whole parish, village and church have long since been eaten away, probably as early as the fourteenth century. All that remains of the parish are a couple of cliff-top fields, but White's Directory of Suffolk records that in 1844 there still existed there the base of an ancient cross called John-a-Lane's Cross. It, too, has disappeared.

Before modern sea defences were erected, Lowestoft, now the major fishing port of East Anglia, suffered severe depredations. A law audit of 1228 records that the place where Lothingland (Lowestoft) market used to be held was eroded by the sea and that the Earl of Salisbury had transferred it to another place at or near Gorleston.

Pakefield

During the 1953 flood disaster, one of the few east coast places to suffer little damage was Lowestoft, where a sturdy new sea wall had been completed during the previous year. This wall was an upgrading of a previous defence which had been useful to Lowestoft in its day, but disastrous to the small town of Pakefield immediately to the south of the fishing port.

According to White's *Directory of Suffolk* (1844), *"the parish consists of 670 acres of land only, having suffered much from the encroachments of the ocean, which has washed away about 70 acres during the last twenty years, together with several houses of*

Newton Church.

*This ancient View of Newton Church
is taken from the original Manuscript in the
Possession of the late Thomas Martin, Esq:
of S.t A. Palgrave, Suffolk, which, with the suite
of the Manor of Newton, ⁊c, in 1734 and all the
Village is now swallowed up by the German
Ocean, many centuries since.*

42. The only record of the lost church of Newton, Norfolk.

the cliff." Between 1844 and 1902, a further 80 acres vanished, and by 1952 almost a hundred more houses had gone down the cliff.

The connection with the sea defences at Lowestoft was simple, for they stopped short at Pakefield Street, and anything to the south of a sea wall on the Suffolk coast is prone to suffer accelerated erosion. The presence of the defences meant that material that would have been produced by erosion there and swept along as beach debris, slowing the sea's encroachment, no longer existed, exposing the Pakefield cliffs to the full erosive force of the sea. The erection of groynes and a sea wall at Lowestoft greatly accelerated Pakefield's demise. Pakefield's independent-minded parish council had rejected Lowestoft's offer of incorporation into the borough at the turn of the century, and that meant missing out on the municipal coastal protection then being erected by its northerly neighbour.

Pakefield did not have long to wait before the folly of their council's decision was made evident. On October 19th, 1 905, there was a severe cliff fall, and the Old Rectory was left marooned on the very edge of the cliff, as was the 30-year old Cliff Hotel. For Pakefield, this was but a foretaste of worse things to come. Shortly after the 1905 cliff fall, the Parish Council changed its corporate mind, seeing that the Lowestoft defences were causing the erosion, and begged that the Lowestoft Corporation should accept the urban part of the parish into the borough, but in January, 1908, their application was refused, and Pakefield's fate was sealed. By then the loss of land since 1900 varied between 130 and 220 feet in depth. By 1929, the inroads of erosion had become so severe that Pakefield Parish Council had erected a series of low groynes along 3,300 feet of the beach. These had the effect of reducing the erosion over a ten year period to a relatively modest 35 feet.

Pakefield finally became incorporated in Lowestoft borough in 1934 and in that year a new sea wall and promenade was begun, but before it could be completed, on December 1st 1936 one of the highest tides for forty years washed away three houses and

43. A cliff fall at Pakefield, south of Lowestoft, when the flimsy sea defences proved inadequate.

44. There were extensive cliff falls at Pakefield in 1905, ripping houses apart, and attracting tourists who bought postcards of photographs of the wreckage that are illustrated here and on the next page.

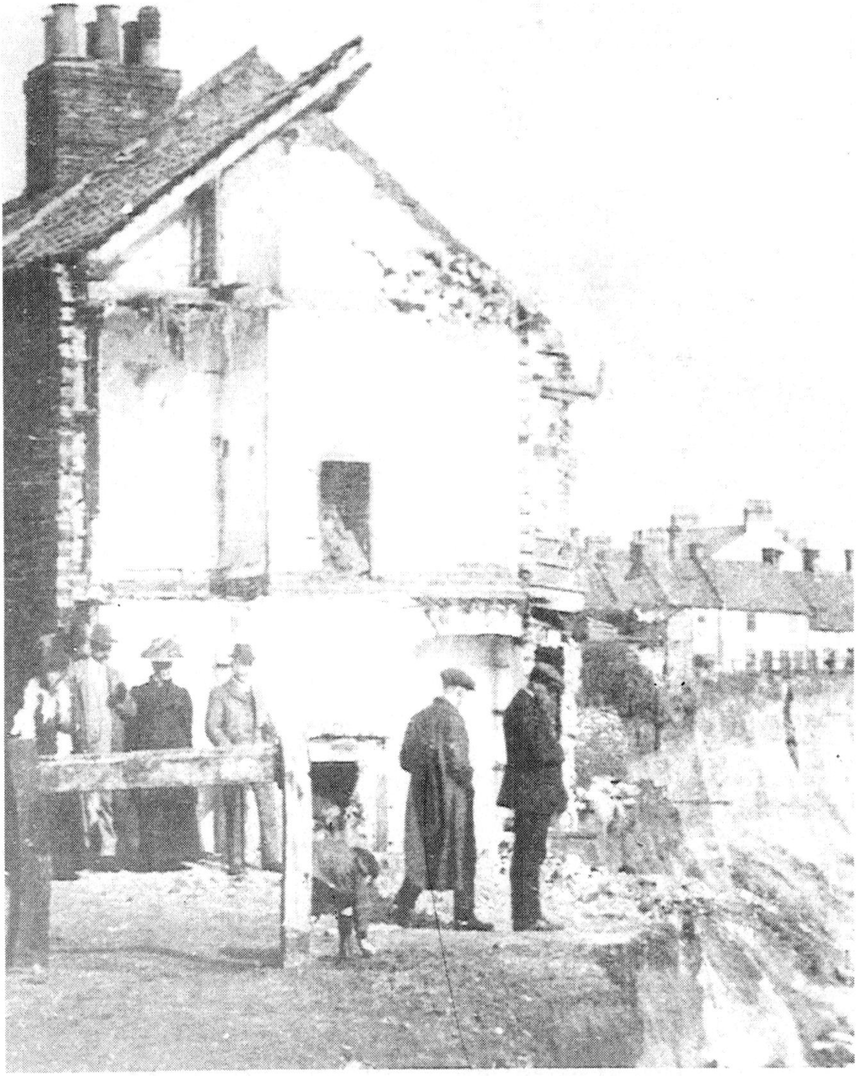

damaged several others beyond repair. Some houses had to be abandoned at a moment's notice as the cliff falls continued in bursts for over three hours, and the whole of Beach Street disappeared for ever. On February 12th-13th, an even higher tide created further mayhem. Backed up by a 70 mph gale, the surge tide ripped away more of the cliffs, and with it more houses.

By the time of the 1938 disaster, Lowestoft Corporation was questioning the wisdom of continuing to build defences along the coast at Pakefield, with the result that all further work was stopped. But during the squabbling in the council chamber in 1939, the erosion continued apace, and the church was left standing at the cliff edge in imminent danger of going 'down the cliff'. This prospect panicked the council into immediately resuming work on the sea wall. Unfortunately, the outbreak of the Second World War meant that only a temporary defence could be erected, one that was a good target for German bombs. On April 21st, 1941, the German Luftwaffe deliberately attacked this makeshift sea wall, and the sea then breached it, dragging away yet more of the cliff, to the effect that erosion between 1940 and 1943 totalled 192 feet. Drastic emergency work was carried out in 1942, but that did little to mitigate the erosive force of the tides.

During the course of half a century, Pakefield was reduced to a mere shadow of its former glory. In old geographies, we read that Easton Bavents was formerly the most easterly part of England, a fame now claimed by Lowestoft. A map of 1575 shows a headland between Lowestoft and Southwold known as Easton Ness, protruding a mile or so into the North Sea and forming the northern boundary of Sole Bay off Southwold. This now-vanished bay was bounded on its southerly flank by another headland, south of Dunwich, and recorded in Ptolemy's map of Britain (1st century AD), in which it is called Exzoye. Easton Ness still existed in 1724, when it was shown on a local map, but the ubiquitous White's *Directory* records in 1844 that the town of Easton Bavents which stood on the cliff was "*a decayed parish on the sea cliff... has now only 10 inhabitants and about 260 acres of*

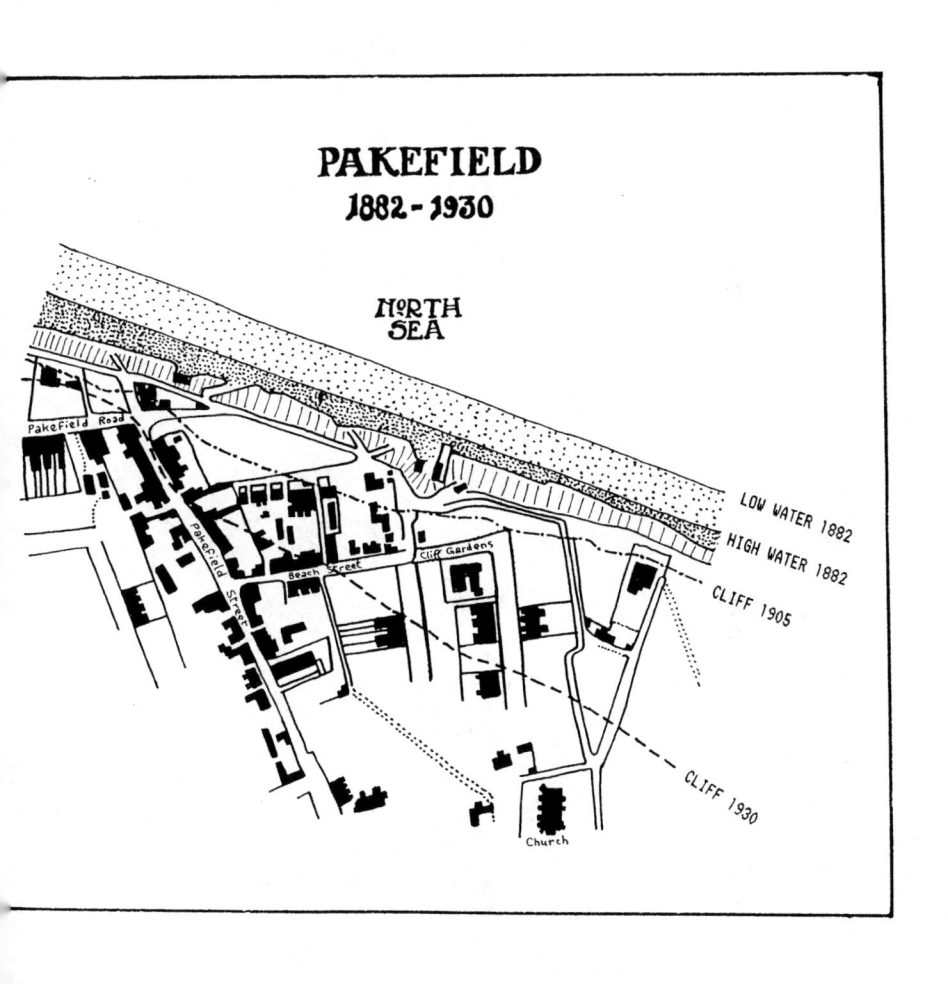

46. The catestrophic erosion of Pakefield, 1882 - 1930.

47. The picturesque Easton Ness was once the most easterly part of Great Britain. Now a mean concrete sea wall marks the furthest east we can go on dry land.

land... Formerly it was an extensive parish, and was returned as having 770 acres of land as late as 1815... a cottage and about 60 acres of land gone down into the sea during the last five years. The church (St Nicholas) was standing in 1638, and had a chapel dedicated to St Margaret, but all vestiges of it are gone..."

Dunwich

Of all the towns around the British coast to be lost to the sea, Dunwich was undoubtedly the largest and most important. Situated in the Hundred of Blything, in the County of Suffolk, Dunwich was at one time a city, the seat of the Bishop of East Anglia. As nominal capital of the Kingdom of East Anglia, Dunwich boasted "*a stone wall and brazen gates, fifty-two churches, chapels, religious houses and hospitals, a king's palace, a mayoral mansion house and a mint.*" The city was situated immediately to the north of a forest, which stretched southwards for seven miles, and was connected to Bury St Edmunds by an old Roman road called the King's Highway.

Antiquaries have long held the belief that Dunwich grew from a Roman station, as it was the focus of several Roman roads. Its name, however, is not derived from the Latin, but from the Anglo Saxon dun, a hill, and wyc, a fort. The final syllable recurs in East Anglia in the names of other important towns such as Norwich and Ipswich. In Saxon times, Dunwich was situated atop a cliff about forty feet high. To the north and west it was defended by palisade-topped earth ramparts, surrounded by a deep ditch. The last traces of these Saxon earthworks were obliterated about the middle of the eighteenth century.

King Sigebert of East Anglia, who introduced Christianity to the land and founded the original University at Cambridge, made Dunwich into an episcopal see by installing Felix of Burgundy as the first Bishop of East Anglia. During his exile on the continent, Sigebert had made the acquaintance of Felix, who had become his spiritual mentor. When Sigebert returned, he installed - Felix whose name is immortalised in the Suffolk port of Felixstowe - as Bishop in AD 636. The first church at Dunwich was built to

48. The medieval seal of the City of Dunwich.

house Felix's services, and he was buried in it in the year 647. Soon after, more churches were erected, dedicated to St Leonard and St John. It is a strange coincidence that a church with the unusual dedication to St Leonard also existed in the lost town of Old Winchelsea in Sussex. At Dunwich, the greatest local event in medieval times was the St Leonard's Fair, which was held in the parish of the same name on the fifth, sixth and seventh of November each year.

In the time of Edward the Confessor, shortly before the Norman conquest, it is recorded that a certain Edric of Saxfield held Dunwich for one manor; there were 120 burgesses, and the town paid an annual tax of ten pounds. At the beginning of the reign of Henry II, Dunwich became a Royal Demesne, according to the chronicler William of Newbury: *"a town of good note abounding with much riches and sundry kinds of merchandise."*. During this period, the town withstood an attack by Robert, Earl of Leicester and his army of Flemish mercenaries. Having over-run Norwich,

Leicester marched to East Anglia's other major city, Dunwich, but after reconnoitring the strong defences, withdrew back into Leicestershire. According to an old manuscript in the British Museum. *"When he came neere and beheld the strength thereof, it was terror and feare unto him to behold it; and soe retired both he and his people."* The remains of the Earl of Leicester's fortified military encampment was formerly visible at Westleton Heath.

Having helped King John in his epic struggle against the Barons, the men of Dunwich were rewarded by a charter making the city a Free Borough. In the tenth year of his reign, John confirmed the charter, adding the rights and privileges of a guild of merchants, and instituted to office of manor which was supported by four sheriffs. Henry III confirmed all of his father's grants to the borough, and bestowed upon the town a lot of land for the construction of a house of the Minor Friars, whose monastic order had just appeared in England. Having once been an episcopal see, Dunwich naturally attracted religious houses. From the twelfth century to the beginning of the fourteenth, it was also an important centre for the Knights Templar, who built a 'Temple' situated near Middlesgate Street, having Duck Street on its north and Convent Garden on its south. Inside the sanctuary of the Temple, comparable in layout with the Temple in London (now one of the Inns of Court of the legal profession), was held a court known as Dunwich Temple Court, held each year on All Saints' Day, November 2nd, with the purpose of collecting due revenues. On the suppression of the order, the Templars' property was turned over to their sister organisation, the Order of St John of Jerusalem, otherwise known as the Knights Hospitaller. They already owned lands in Dunwich, and this takeover consolidated their position as the foremost monastic order in the city. Like other English monastic orders, the Hospitalers came to an ignominious end when Henry VIII decided to dispossess them. But by his day, Dunwich was itself being dispossessed by the sea.

In addition to the two monastic houses of the Templars and Hospitalers, Dunwich had two Priories belonging respectively to the Grey Friars and the Black Friars. The Grey Friars' Priory

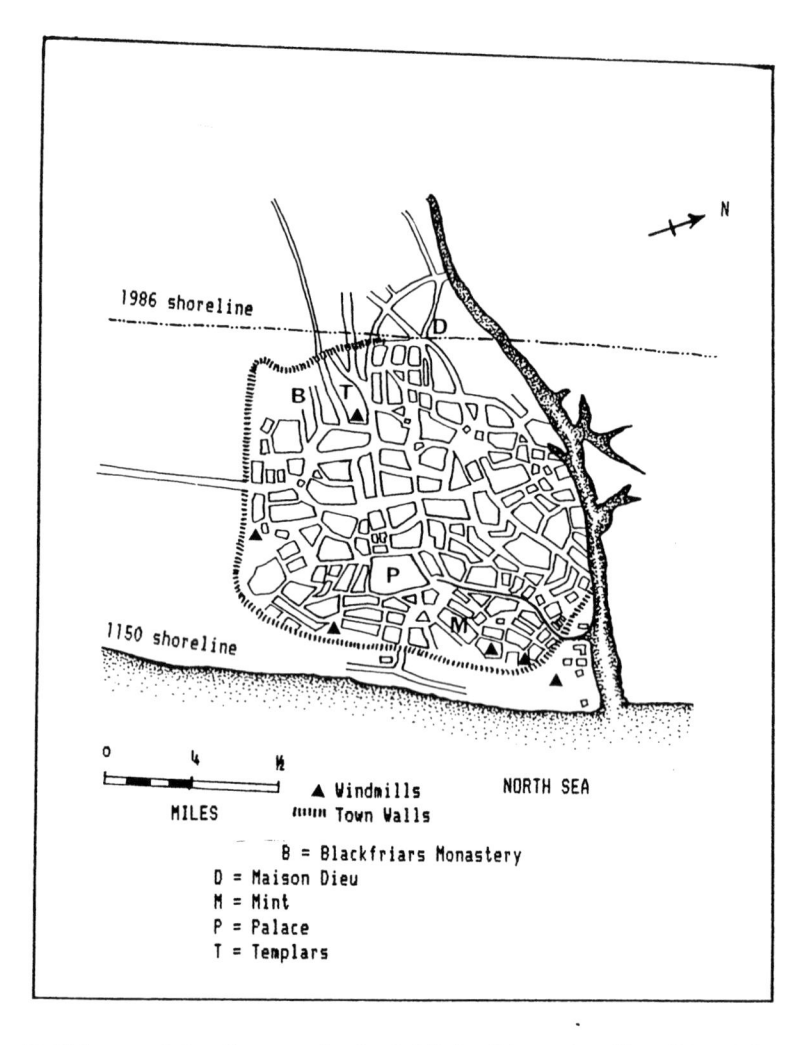

49. 836 years of shoreline recession has left little of the ancient City of Dunwich

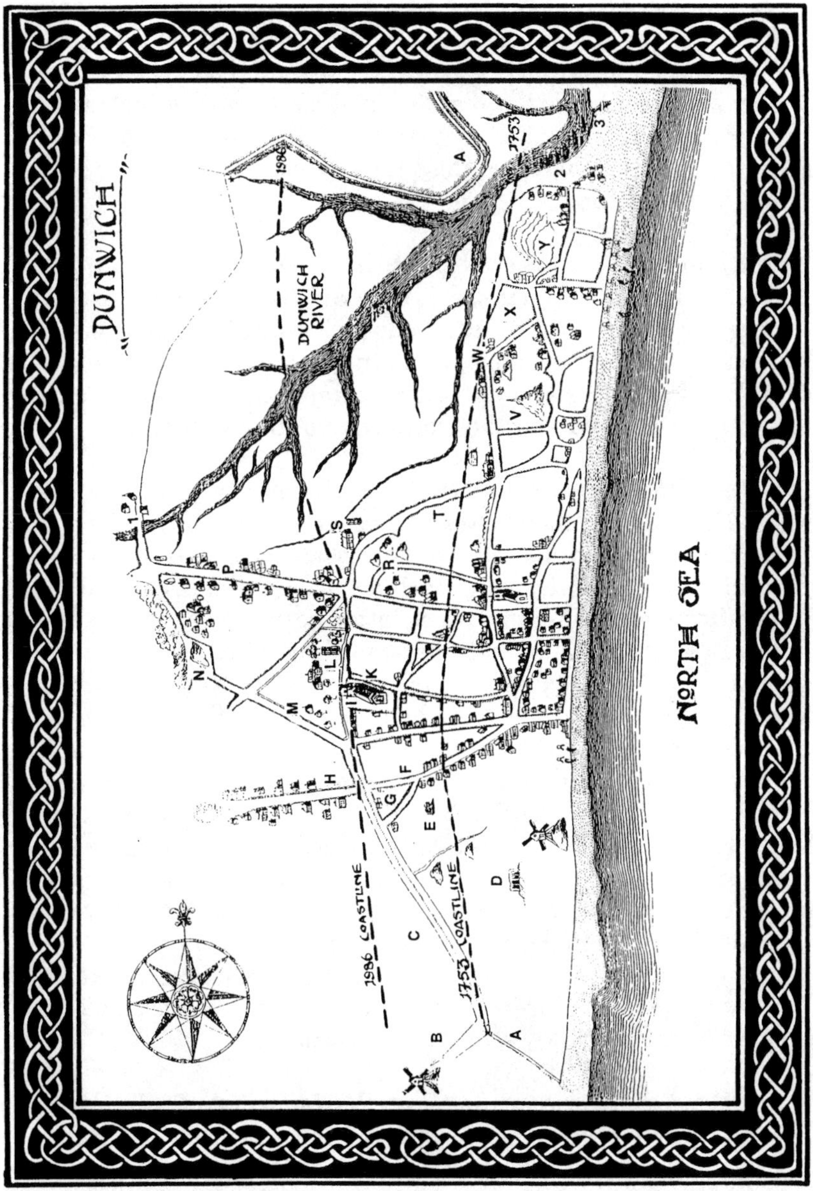

DUNWICH
DUNWICH RIVER
NORTH SEA
1986 COASTLINE
1753 COASTLINE
1986
1753

was built into the town wall. It had three gates, two oriented to the west, the other east. The Priory of the Dominicans or Black Friars was founded by Sir Roger de Holish and seems to have been a favourite burial-place for crusaders and other military worthies of the town. Like the Grey Friars' establishment, the Black Friars' was encompassed by a substantial stone wall. This Priory is of geomantic interest, for in 1259 it was the centre of a demarcation dispute between the Chapters of Dunwich and Norwich over the bounds of their jurisdiction over local convents, tithes and preaching.

The dispute was referred to William of Nottingham, the boundaries expert of their order. He stated at the Convocation of Gloucester that their convents' boundaries should be determined naturally by their respective counties' rivers, excepting at Mendham and Rushworth, which straddle the rivers. These villages were to be under the jurisdiction of Dunwich alone.

Dunwich sported another convent of uncertain allegiance, subordinate to the monastery at Eye in Suffolk. In addition to these monastic establishments there were parish churches and several large hospitals, which included the Maison Dieu and the Leper Hospital of St James. This latter hospital was founded by John, Earl Moreton, later to become King John. This hospital gave its name to the town's main street, St James's Street, which was the site of an annual fair held on the saint's patronal day and the day following. Most of the town's shops were in St James's Street, which ran inland from the waterfront. Another major thoroughfare was King's Street, which joined the rampart south of the town. To the north of Dunwich was the entrance into the harbour, protected on its northern side by a pier made of wooden piles whose remains were visible until about 200 years ago. Ancient chroniclers depict Dunwich as a flourishing and wealthy seaport, and had the sea been less harsh, no doubt today the town would have been a major east coast seaport with all the modern facilities. However, that was not to be.

As early as the Norman conquest, the *Domesday Book* records that two pieces of land at Dunwich, taxed in the time of Edward

51. Gardner's 1753 engraving of the remians of Dunwich.

the Confessor had been washed away by the tides. This early piece of coastal erosion did not daunt the people of Dunwich, for its increasing prosperity seemed to have no limit until one fateful day in the early fourteenth century. On January 14th, 1328, a storm altered the configuration of the sandbanks off Dunwich, blocking the harbour mouth. A rapid build-up of riverwater behind the new sand-bar forced its way through at a new opening, forming a completely new harbour. This in turn succumbed to the sea's unpredictable changes during the reign of Henry IV.

This time, the Corporation set to work to dig another harbour, which endured until another disastrous storm in 1464. When this in turn was swept away, yet another harbour mouth, known as Hummerton's Cut, was excavated, but this altered the tidal flow which soon caused the formation of a treacherous sandbank known as Passely Sands. Many ships were wrecked on this sandbank, and eventually the mariners refused to use Dunwich because navigation was too hazardous. By 1589, trade had declined to the point where the construction of a new port was imperative, but a legal wrangle with nearby Southwold and Walberswick prevented any action at all while the protracted case was heard. The other two towns dug their own unauthorised haven, which resulted in ten years' litigation with Dunwich. When everything had finally been sorted out, the Dunwich Corporation found itself almost bankrupted by legal expenses, and too short of funds to build the essential new haven mouth.

By the time Dunwich suffered its financial crisis, there was an even more serious threat to the very existence of Dunwich. By 1349, a large portion of the city had already been swept away, comprising over 400 houses and several mills. By 1385, the ancient Saxon church of St Felix and its cell of ascetes the churches of St Martin, St Nicholas and St Leonard had all gone 'down the cliff'.

By the fifteenth century, Dunwich was in the unenviable position of losing a church a decade into the sea, and by 1540, the town's inhabitants were actively demolishing their sacred buildings

SALVAGE AT DUNWICH.

ENGRAVED BY R. PATERSON FROM A DRAWING BY W. E. F. BRITTEN.

before the sea could claim them for its own. The parishioners of St John's and St Peter's tore down their churches in that year. In the chancel of St John's they found a large gravestone covering a tomb which contained the corpse of a man, which crumbled to dust upon being exposed to the air. According to Weever's Ancient Funeral Monuments, written in 1631, *"When St John's church was taken down, there lay a very faire gravestone in the chancel, and when it was raised and taken up, next under the same gravestone was a hollow stone, hollowed after the fashion of a man, for a man to lye in; and therein a man lying with a pair of bootes upon his legges, the forepart of the feet of them peicked, after a strange fashion, and a pair of chalices of course metal lying upon his breast, the which was thought to be one of the Bishops of Dunwiche, but when they touched and stirred the same dead body it fell and went all to powder and dust."*

By now the old city was doomed. In 1608, the old high road to the sea was swept away, and a few years later the foundations of the Temple and its ancillary buildings *"yielded to the irresistable force of the undermining surges."* In 1677 the inhabitants of the now depleted town fled as the market place went down the cliff, and three years later all of the buildings north of Maison Dieu Lane were demolished. In 1702, following the by-now familiar pattern of Dunwich, another church was *"obliged to be broken down."* The Town Hall collapsed two years later, and in 1729, St Peter's cemetery was ripped asunder. As the remains of their forebears went down the cliff, the inhabitants had gathered together, cursing the sea with oaths and clenched fists; but more than puny human protests were needed to halt the inexorable march of coastal erosion.

The last major blow came in December 1739/1740. A storm. which had continued unabated for several days, ripped away the great church together wlth huge portions of the now-diminished town. St Nicholas's and St Francis's cemeteries were undermined, and the bones of the dead, mingled with their shattered memorials, were strewn about the storm-torn beach. The Cock and Hen Hills, which had been upwards of forty feet high, were levelled during the mighty tempest, and to all intents

53. Gardner's 1753 engraving of the last fragments of the Greyfriars' Priory.

54. Fragments of Old Dunwich buildings used as furniture for customers in a garden of a Dunwich public house.

and purposes the history of Dunwich as a town was ended. All that remained were a handful of cottages. This storm was notable also in that it uncovered the roots of a great number of trees, the last remnants of the mighty East Wood, writing the epitaph on an era.

Visiting the remains of Dunwich shortly afterwards, Thomas Gardner of the Society of Antiquaries of London wrote: '*I beheld the Remains of the Rampart; some tokens of Middlegate; the Foundations of Downfalled Edifices and tottering Fragments of Noble Structures, Remains of the Dead exposed, and naked Wells divested of the Cround about them, by the Waves of the Sea! divers Coins, several Mill-Hills, and part of the Old Key.*" His researches recovered the most complete street plan of Dunwich still existing. On Februrary 5th, 1753, Gardner published the plan, which showed the general disposition of the port of Dunwich and its street layout as existing in the year 1587, along with engravings of several of the churches then extant. His plan lists the following streets and landmarks of Dunwich: The Rampart, Convent Garden, Sea Field, Black Friers (sic), Temple, Duck Street, Middle Gate, Mid Gate Street, All Saint's Church, Scotts Lane, Grey Friers, Maison Dieu Hills, Maison Dieu Hospital, Maison Dieu Lane, Cock Hills, St Francis's Chapel, St Francis's Meadow, Hen Hills, King's Holm, Deering Bridge and the Old Key (sic). By the mid eighteenth century, Dunwich had become merely a tourist attraction, visited by antiquaries and melancholy poets reflecting on the transience of "*sublunary things*".

Dunwich continued to send two members to Parliament at Westminster until the abolition of 'rotten boroughs' in the Reform Bill in 1832. Of latter-day parliamentary interest is the Dunwich member in the Parliaments of 1710, 1713 and up to 1749, Sir George Downing, whose name is preserved in Downing Street, site of the Prime Minister's residence. After 1832, the last token recognition of this erstwhile great borough was abolished, and the sea found itself eating away mainly farmland.

149

South of Dunwich is Aldeborough, which has had to move inland to avoid the same fate as its illustrious neighbour. Over the centuries, the town was moved progressively westwards, until the unfortunate townsfolk found themselves at their municipal boundary. The old town once lay a quarter of a mile seawards of the present place, and as late as 1559 was protected by a belt of sand dunes. Once these were breached, erosion was inevitable, and in 1886 it was calculated that there were 24 feet of water over the site of the old town.

Essex has suffered relatively little coastal losses, being in a less violent part of the coast. In former times, the seaport of Orwell at the mouth of the river of the same name was the main port in that part of the country. Of it nothing now remains but West Rocks off Harwich, which, before the construction of sturdy sea walls during the last century was in danger of following Orwell beneath the waves. Before the defences halted the erosion, it was feared that Harwich was soon to become an island as a prelude to its ultimate destruction.

To the south of Orwell is Walton-on-the-Naze, a town whose very name is derived from its sea wall. Despite the wall, the town formerly extended much further to the east. The destruction of land near Walton, whose Naze is still seriously threatened by coastal attrition, gave rise to one of those quaint anomalies beloved of ancient English institutions. Formerly at Walton there was an endowment of land for the expenses of one of the prebends of St Paul's but when the sea engulfed it, the office or gift came to be called *Praebenda consumpta per mare* (The Prebendary consumed by the sea). This loss of revenue to the point of nothingness by coastal erosion was paralleled by another farm in the same parish, purchased by the Governors of Queen Anne's Bounty in 1739 for the expenses of Holy Trinity rectory in Chichester. It dwindled rapidly much to the rector's disadvantage.

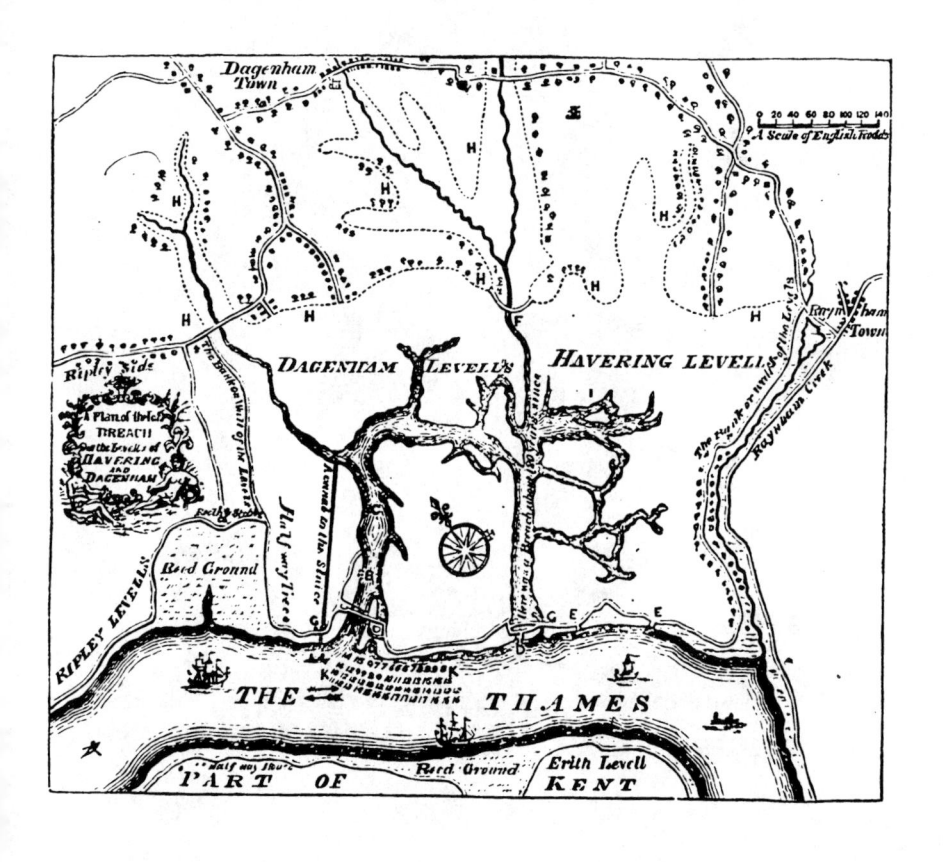

55. *Contempoary map of the Dagenham Breach.*

56. Photomontage issued by the Greater London Council in the 1970s, giving an impression of tyhe flood disaster threatening London.

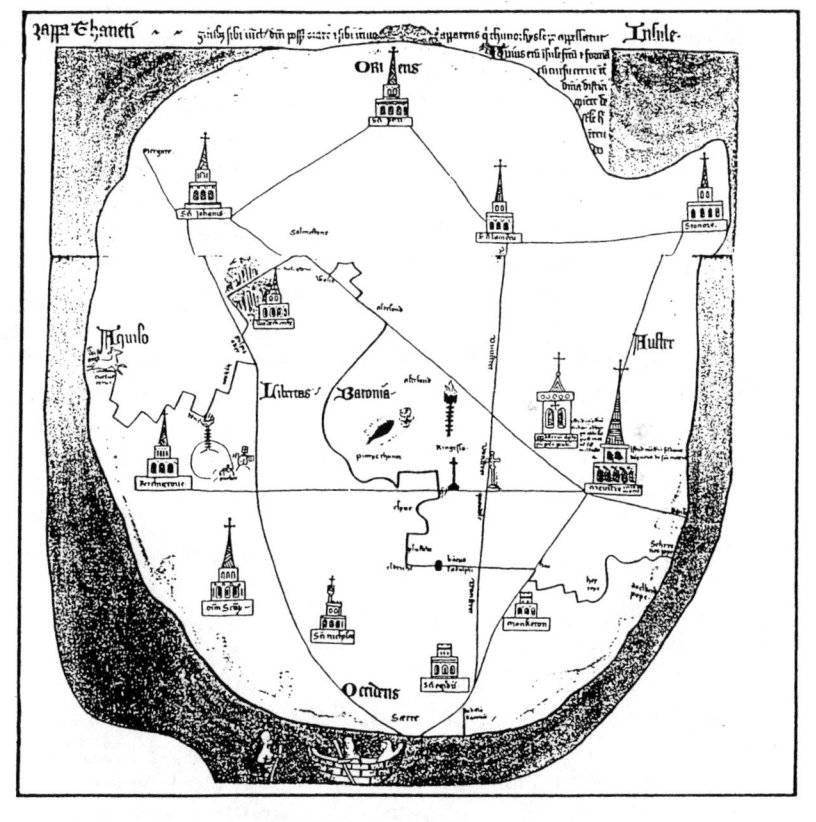

57. *Medieval map of the Island of Thanet, showing its division into four quarters with a cross at the central crossroads.*

The Dagenham Breach

The Thames estuary has been the site of many incursions over the years. Plumstead Marsh was overflowed in 1279, and the bank opposite in 1522, not being reclaimed until 1606. At Dagenham, there were 'breaches' in 1376, when the nuns of Dagenham had to flee to higher ground, and in 1621, when the Dutch engineer Cornelius Vermuijden was employed to 'inn' Dagenham Creek to prevent further floods.

The most notable incursion there was the famous 'Dagenham Breach' which occurred on December 17, 1707, after a very high spring tide coincided with a north-easterly gale. A sixteen-foot hole was battered in the defences, but nobody bothered to repair it; the constant inwash and outwash of the tides widened the gap to 100 yards and deepened it to thirty feet. A thousand acres of land in the Dagenham area and Hornchurch Levels were flooded, passing up the west by Chequer's Lane, branching out northwards through Dagenham village, two miles from the river, and up the course of the River Bream. Attempts were made to block the breach. An old government ship, the Lion, was filled with rubble and scuttled in the breach, but it was broken up by the following high tide, and the channel was then found to be twenty feet deeper than before. In 1714, the scour of materials from the Dagenham and Havering Levels was causing large banks to build up in the Thames itself, creating a hazard to navigation which caused the government to impose a tax on shipping for ten years to pay for the necessary works.

In his book *An account of the stopping of Dagenham Breach* published in 1721, Captain Perry detailed the methods he used to successfully block the breach. At a hired yard in Rotherhithe his workmen prefabricated 'dove-tailed' fir piles. These were rammed into the bed of the breach at low tide, and, when complete, banks of earth were raised on the foundations. Associated embankments and a relieving canal were cut. Despite a near-disaster in 1717, when a high tide almost washed away the work, the breach was finally closed and the work completed in 1720. During the works, the contractors unearthed Moorlogg. a vein of different kinds of woods, including yew, hazel and

58. *Seventeenth century map, showing the location of Reculver.*

'brushwood', possibly part of the 'submerged forest' of which remains have been found in the Plumstead Marshes.

Reculver

During the Roman occupation, military engineers built a series of castles along the eastern coast of Britain to act as strong points in the defence against Saxon attack. One of these 'Forts of the Saxon Shore' was Regulbium - now the Kentish Reculver - which at the time of its construction was over two miles from the sea. Like the sister fort at Gariannonum (Burgh Castle by Great Yarmouth), the Saxons, whom the forts were built to repel, took over Reculver shortly after their accession to power in the nation. When St Augustine's mission came to Britain, King Ethelbert of Kent handed over his royal palace at Canterbury so that the saint could construct a new cathedral there. In the year 597, the king retired to the Old Roman defences at Reculver, which he made the seat of Kentish government. Reculver remained the regal seat until AD 669, when King Egbert, Ethelbert's grandson, presented the fort and palace to a Benedictine monk named Bassa. The monk converted the fort into a monastery, continuing the Benedictine tradition whereby that order held the key centres of power in Christendom. The church of the new monastery was dedicated to St Mary the Virgin, and was built almost at the geometric centre of the old fort, which was renamed Racult Minster.

The monastery flourished and continued to expand until the ninth century, when Danish raiders wiped it out. In 949, the refounded monastery and its estates were granted by King Eadred to Christ Church at Canterbury. During the early post-conquest period, the church was expanded and the two famous 63-foot landmark towers, now the only remaining part of the building, were erected. But although expansion was taking place, the sea was creeping closer and closer. When Leland visited the place in about 1535, he found the church standing "*within a quarter of a mile or a little more*" from the sea. In 1783, the sea undermined and destroyed the north side of the Roman curtain wall, and began to erode the land inside.

59. Reculver Church in the late 18th century.

SEA

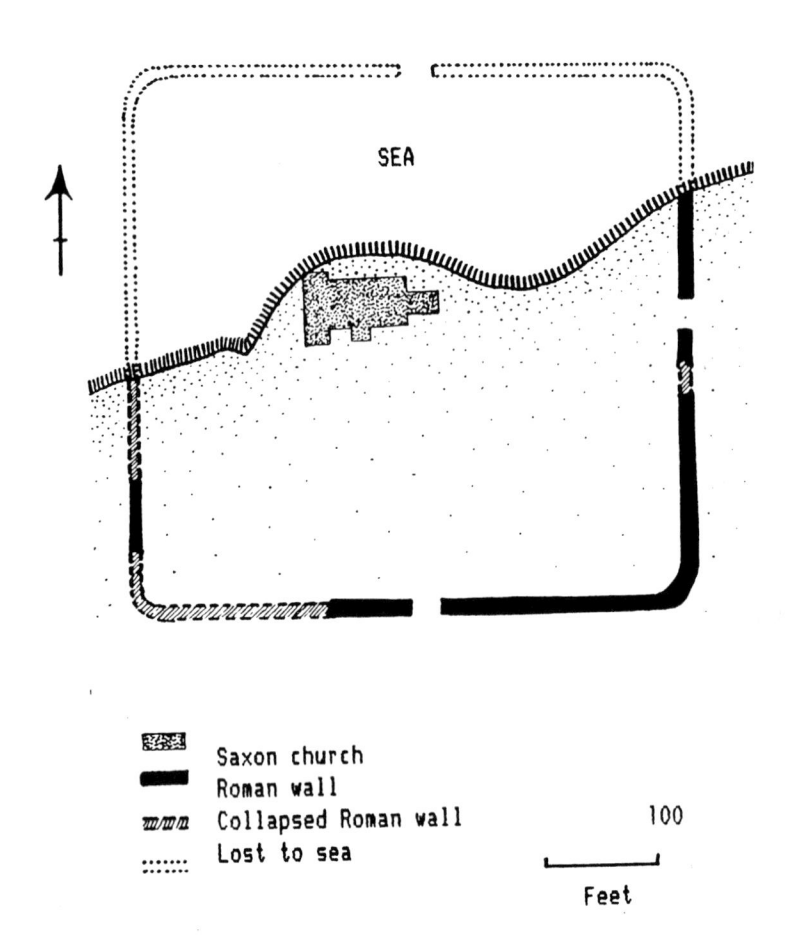

▨	Saxon church
▬	Roman wall
▨▨▨	Collapsed Roman wall
....	Lost to sea

100

Feet

60. Reconstruction of the Roman fort of reculver.

By 1800, the sea was approaching the churchyard walls, a separate enclosure parallel to but within the Roman walls, and the church had fallen into a serious state of disrepair. According to the historian Freeman, the churchyard was entire as late as 1805, with a highway, between the churchyard wall and cliff, broad enough to admit a carriage, if anyone had been foolhardy to drive one along such a dangerously unsafe track. In 1808, a Parish Meeting resolved to demolish the ruined church, and to re-erect it about a mile inland, on the site of the present church. "*In 1809*", wrote Freeman, "*the distance from the north angle of the tower to the edge of the cliff, is reduced to five yards only.*" The towers were, however, important landmarks for mariners, and their demolition would have seriously hampered navigation, so before the Parish Council's decision to demolish could be implemented, Trinity House purchased them, and with additional protection, they have survived until the present day.

Like many lost towns and villages, Reculver has a sea storm legend. This one is not the usual spectral bells, however, but states that on stormy nights the cries of babies can be heard on the wind. It is strange to relate that during the 1960s, ex cavations in the Roman fort at Reculver revealed a number of infants' skeletons, probably the remains of babies buried alive as foundation sacrifices.

Goodwin Sands (Lomea)

Off the Kentish coast lies one of the most notorious of the English Channel's many treacherous sandbanks - the Goodwin Sands. As many as 50,000 mariners are believed to have perished in shipwrecks there, but before the disastrous Martinmas Flood of 1099, the sands were a fertile tract of land of many thousand acres "*of goodlie pasture*", formerly the property of Earl Godwin, father of the ill-fated King Harold ll who died at Hastings in 1066.

The sands are about ten miles long by seven wide, and are exposed at low tide, but before the 1099 flood were the fertile island of Lomea. No scheme has ever been advanced to reclaim

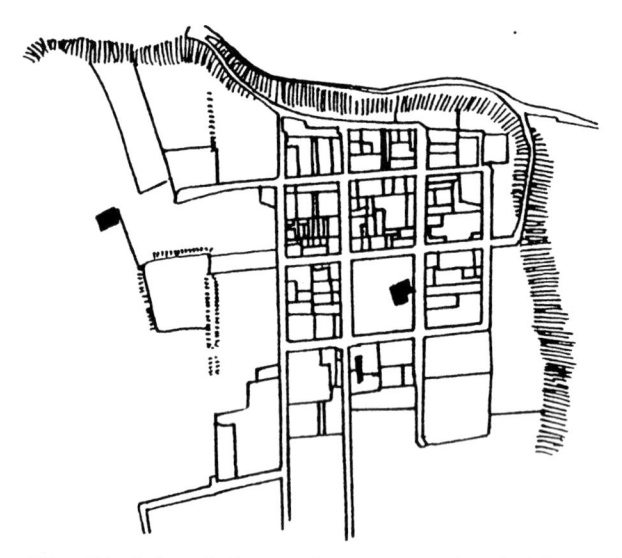

61. Plan of New Winchelsea, built according to geomantic principles to r4eplace the old town, lost to the sea.

the district as pasture, although their provenance as former land was shown in 1817 by engineers of the Trinity Board, who carried out trial borings on the bank for the possible erection of a lighthouse. They discovered that the bank consists of fifteen feet of sand, resting on blue clay, finally with a bedrock of chalk, the material underlying the whole English Channel.

The Isle of Sheppey, which one day may go the way of Lomea, was formerly much larger than at present. The eminent geologist Lyell noted that the cliffs on the north side of the island were eroded away at a rate of 50 acres between 1810 and 1830, and that the coastal church of Minster was in the centre of the island in 1780. Further along the coast, erosion has made Herne Bay a bay in name only. Like the lost bay between Easton Ness and Covehithe Mass in Suffolk, this bay has been reduced to a more or less straight profile by the erosion of its two headlands.

Dover and Folkestone

Dover, the nearest English town to continental Europe, lost considerable territory in historic times. Shakespeare's Cliff, so-named after a passage in *King Lear*, was diminishing in height yearly before the construction of sea defences, as the summit slopes inland. In Shakespeare's time, when the cliff was less eroded and thus much higher, it was an even more impressive sight than at present. A major landslip in 1772, occasioned by an earthquake, is reputed to have taken a massive slice off of the cliff, altering further the topography of Dover. Since Roman times. the port has altered drastically, as the harbour was originally in an estuary between lofty chalk cliffs, long since eroded.

The present town of Folkestone is not the original, for that has long since gone. Old Folkestone was built "*on a high cliff, close to the sea-shore*", but that since is now a good half-mile offshore of the present harbour. In the sixteenth century, Leland wrote of Old Folkestone that "*The Town shore be al Iyklihod is mervelusly wasted with the violens of the se; yn so much that there they say one Paroche chyrch of Our Lady, and another of St Paula is clene destroy'd and etin by the se.*"

In 1716, a local writer noted that within then living memory the cliff had been eroded to the distance of ten rods (165 feet), and that year a major landslip took more. This altered the topography so drasti cally that "*houses became visible from certain points at sea, and from particular spots on the sea cliffs, from whence they could not be seen previously.*" Eyewitnesses saw several acres of clifftop land slide forwards in a body, like a ship being launched. Several major falls have taken place there since.

Old Winchelsea

Although the present town of Winchelsea is separated from the sea by a mile of low-lying meadows and shingle banks, the result of the sea's recession since medieval times, it has not receded far enough to uncover the remains of the once-mighty seaport that lay three miles distant from its namesake. The original

Winchelsea was situated on a low-lying island six miles northeast of Fairlight Cliff. Commanding the mouth of the River Rother, Old Winchelsea and its twin lost village of Promehill stood, as does Lydd, upon the ancient and seemingly stable shingle spit. Old Winchelsea's antiquity has been hotly disputed. Camden believed it to postdate the Roman occupation, whilst Johnson's Atlas declares it have been a city in Roman times.

Gough's edition of Camden's *Britannia* calls it Portus Novus, a Roman port, but all of these fine assertions may merely betray faulty scholarship or wishful thinking. The position of the old town, however, is recorded meticulously in Dugdale's *History of Embanking*, where it is placed immediately to the east of the easterly pier head of Rye Harbour, adjoining the Camber Farm Estate. In his preface to *The History of Cornwall*, published in 1724, Norden asserts that Old Winchelsea's "ruins thereof lie under the waves three miles within the high sea."

What could have been so important about this island town to qualify it for the attentions of so many antiquarian luminaries? Its position. At the time of the Norman Conquest, Old Winchelsea was the most convenient port for communication with France. According to Norden, at its height Old Winchelsea was a town of "*great trade and accompt*," having a population of about 5,000. Its strategic importance can be gauged from the fact that William the Conqueror pre-empted an English revolt against the Norman yoke by unexpectedly landing there on December 7, 1067. This strategic importance was officially recognised during the twelfth century when Hastings, the westernmost of the famous Cinque Ports Confederation - together with Romney, Hythe, Sandwich and Dover - requested that Winchelsea and Rye should be admitted as members. Old Winchelsea was at that time larger and more important than Rye, possessing three churches dedicated respectively to St Thomas the Martyr, St Giles and St Leonard.

Having gained this important privilege, Winchelsea went straight ahead and abused it. The townsmen, who were under the jurisdiction of the foreign abbey of Fecamp, in France, felt that they owed allegiance to nobody but themselves. Ships from the port actively and openly practised piracy, plundering the ships of foreigner and English alike. Under the protection of Simon de Montfort, Earl of Leicester, they attacked passing shipping. it was said that the men of Winchelsea gave no quarter; they cast overboard the crews of every ship they met, regardless of nationality, and their crimes became so serious that official complaints were made to the English parliament by representatives of foreign mercantile cities including Ypres, Brugge and Köln.

Annoyed by foreign pressure, King Henry iii resolved to bring the town directly under his own control In 1247 *"for the better defence of the realm"*, he forcibly exchanged the towns of Winchelsea and Rye with the Abbey of Fecamp for less strategic lands elsewhere in England. Hastings and St Leonards, towns of lesser importance, remained the Abbey's possessions. Despite this direct rule, piracy, a lucrative trade if ever there was one, continued much as before. Finally, in 1266, Prince Edward took Old Winchelsea by storm and butchered all of the leading townsmen who had formerly made their living by piracy. The rest he spared, and granted them very lenient terms of surrender.

But already the sea was taking its toll. In 1236 the first major marine incursion occurred at Old Winchelsea, when the town was flooded for a while. In 1251, a far more serious inundation took place. An ancient Winchelsea chronicle records *"On the first day of October, the moon, upon her change appearing ex ceeding red and swelled, began to show tokens of the great tempest of wind that followed, which was so huge and mighty, both by land and sea, the like had not been lightly known and seldom, or rather never, heard of by men then alive. The sea forced, contrary to his natural course, flowed twice without eb bing, yielding such a roaring that the same was heard (not without great wonder) a tar distance from the shore. Moreover, the same sea appeared in the dark of the night to burn, as it had been on fire, and the waves to strive and fight together... At Winchelsea, besides other hurt that was done in bridges, mills, breaks and banks, there were 300*

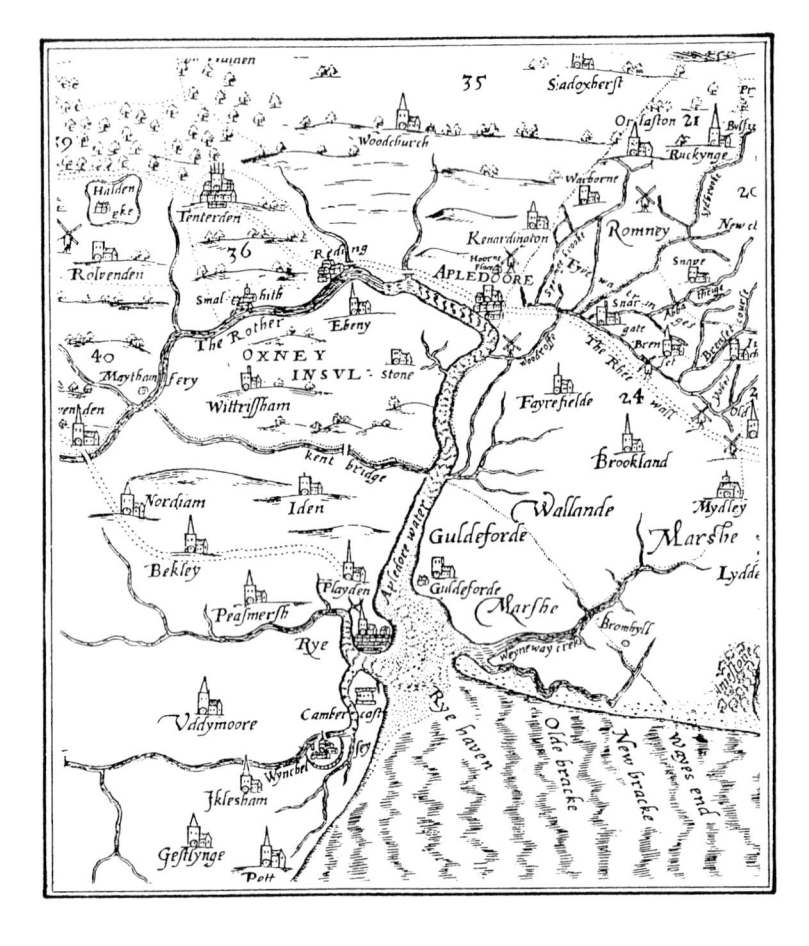

62. Seventeenth century record of a sea battle showing the town of Brighthelmstone.

houses and some churches drowned with the high rising of the water course."

Prayers for mercy were offered after this catastrophe, for the priesthood saw it as God's retribution for the foul deeds of the town's pirates. The town was greatly weakened by this inundation, and after the attack by Prince Edward in 1266, piracy was suppressed, and the Jews, who had settled at Old Winchelsea under the protection of Simon de Montfort, were summarily deported. A bare nineteen years was now to pass before the old town was totally obliterated. On February 4th, 1287, the Vigil of St Agatha, a sudden inroad of the sea wiped out all before it. One ancient French chronicle notes "*On the Second of the Nones of February, the sea at the Isle of Thanet rose and swelled so high and in the Marsh of Romenal, that it brake all the walls and drowned all the grounds; so that from the Great Wall of Appledore as far as Winchelsea, towards the south and west, all the land lay under the water lost.*"

"*In the fearful crash and inundation of 1287*", wrote Montague Burrows in 1888, "*the old half-ruined town was entirely swept away; the course of the River Rother was changed and with it the whole face of the Romney coast. For many centuries no one has been able to point to any particular spot with certainty and say 'Here stood Winchelsea'.*" The River Rother was blocked at its mouth, and the whole pattern of the coastline, and with it the tidal flow systems, was abruptly altered. The town of Winchelsea was swept away, and the new tidal patterns soon scoured away the old shingle bank upon which it had stood.

This had been imminent for several years, for in about 1280, King Edward 1, *Rex et Bastidor*, had visited Old Winchelsea to inspect the decayed town and to select the site for a replacement. As a trading centre with Gascony it was too valuable to be completely abandoned, so the King's geomants were sent out to select a favourable site for its replacement. They chose the Hill of Igham, three miles or so from the old town, and commenced purchasing the land. To oversee the layout of the new town, Edward called in Henry le Waleys, sometime Lord Mayor of

London and Mayor of Bordeaux, and Itier Bouchard, a noted builder of the French new towns known as bastides. These bastides, like the new towns of that period, were laid out on the grid pattern. Having drawn up the plans, surveyors were sent to the Hill of Igham to lay out the rectilinear grid of streets which still survives to this day. The town was divided into 39 'quarters', rectangular plots varying from one and a half to three and a quarter acres in area, defined by eight streets. The 'burgage plots' allocated to landowners from the old town were designed to be, as near as possible, equal in area to those of the destroyed town. The layout of Winchelsea remains today in a reduced form as a prime example of the geomantic town planning of the thirteenth century; an ingenious layout whose complexities are still being studied by geomantic researchers.

When Old Winchelsea was finally overwhelmed, the old Forest of Dimsdale on the coast, which extended westward to Hastings and beyond, was lost. Gradual coastal attrition removed this valuable forest, for by the time of Richard II we find the following reference in Shakespeare's *Richard II.* (Act 3) "...*a certain way and marsh called Dymsdale, between the towns of Winchelsea and Hastings, which way and marsh were destroyed and overwhelmed by the sea.*" At the turn of this century, the remains of a wood was still visible at Pett at low water during spring tides. Parts of oak, beech and fir trees were identified, and it is still common to encounter roots and limbs of forest trees whenever dykes are cut along that stretch of coastline.

Like the present Winchelsea, the modern Hastings is not the original. In ancient times, Old Hastings possessed a good harbour, and a pier, destroyed in Elizabethan times during a storm. On the foreshore, the remains of the forest of Dimsdale were long visible. Embedded in a black deposit, branches, trunks and roots of forest trees, along with hazel-nuts in a near-perfect state of preservation, have turned up. Between Hastings and Pevensey Bay, erosion continued at a disastrous rate. In the last century, the tide carried away Martello towers less than forty years after their erection during the Napoleonic Wars. Beachy Head and the adjoining cliffs, the product of massive erosion

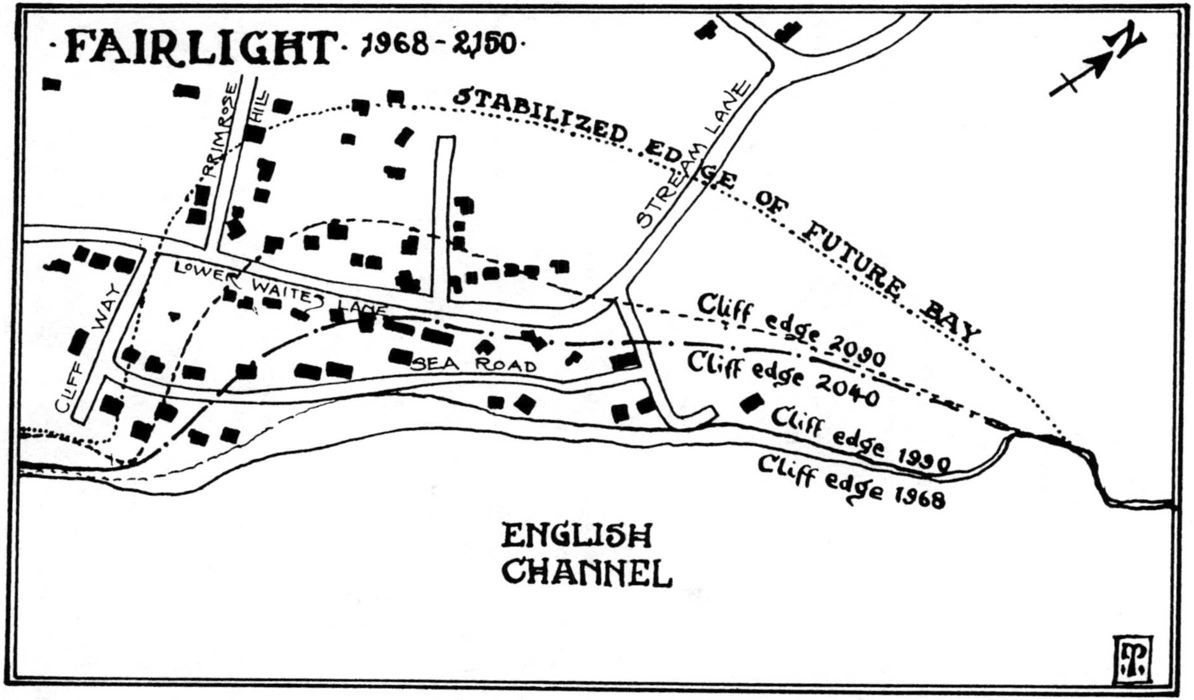

63. *The developing Bay of Fairlight, Sussex.*

after the separation of Britain from the European mainland, have always been the scene of spectacular and dangerous falls. One notable collapse occurred in 1813, when a mass of chalk 300 feet in length and 80 feet in breadth, suddenly fell into the sea from the famous promontory.

On the Pevensey Levels, the villages of Willingdon and Northeye have gone beneath the sea. In former times, the Pevensey Levels were characterised by seven high masses of rock- 'sea stacks' - standing separate from the cliff. Known originally as the Seven Charleses, they gradually succumbed to the inexorable tide. When two had vanished, they became known as the Five Charleses, and gradually, like the 'ten green bottles', they grew fewer and fewer in number until but one, 'The Charleses', remained.

Brighthelmstone

The present seaside town of Brighton owes its eminence to the fashionable attentions of the Prince Regent in the early nineteenth century, yet before it was graced with royal patronage, Brighthelmstone, as it was then known, was nothing more than a small fishing village. By the time of its Regency splendour, however, the town of Brighton was not on the same site as its lowly predecessor.

In *Unknown Brighton*, published in 1926, George Aitchison wrote, "*Who knows of Brighthelmstone, the fishing town underneath the sea? What do we know today about the original Brighton, the fishing town of some 600 houses... utterly washed away?*" Aitchison surmised that the site of the old town was at the point where the sea is now shoulder-high on a shallow bar beyond which it suddenly deepens.

In *Old Brighton, Old Hove, Old Preston* (1937), Frederick Harrison and James Sharp North gave what they believed to be the position of old Brighthelmstone. They recounted the local tradition that there was formerly a spit of land that ran into the sea forming a creek extending into Pool Valley and the Steyne,

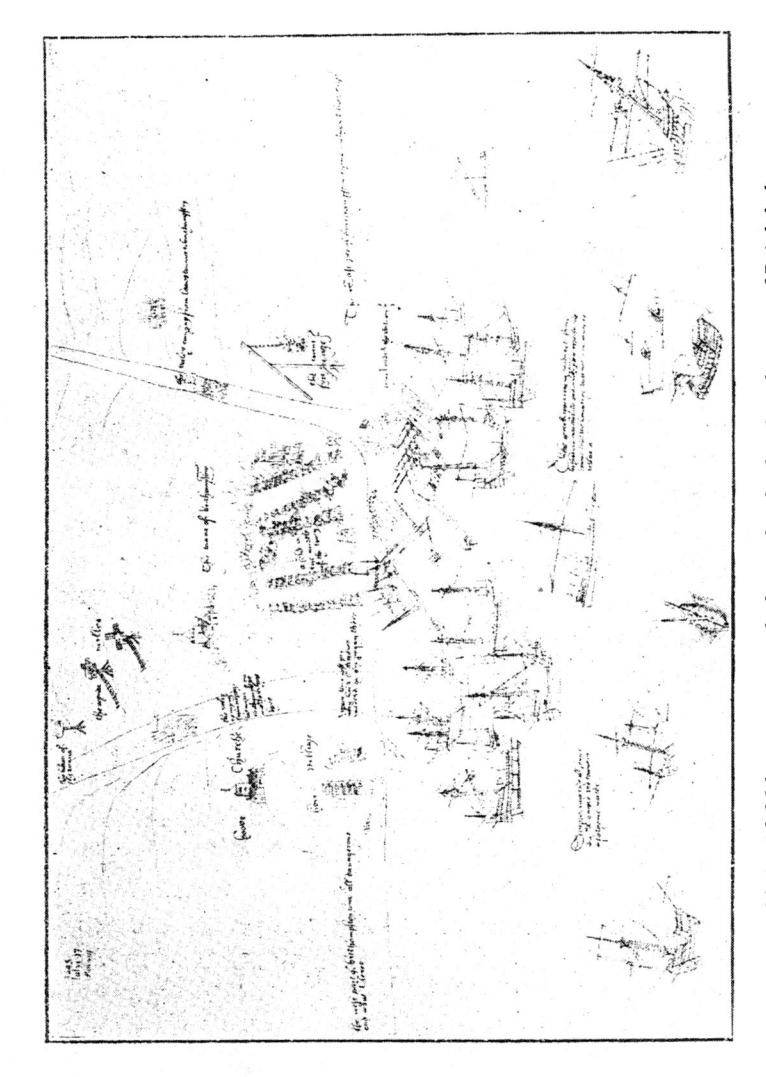

64. A mid-16th century record of a sea battle showing the town of Brighthelmstone.

65. Volk's Railway, at Brighton, built in 1883, in rough weather. This line, first built in 1883 still runs in 1997.

usable as a safe anchorage. The present Brighton grew up along the banks of the small creek, now remembered only in the name Pool Valley, the present bus station.

Of Brighthelmstone, little documentary evidence remains. In his *Book of Knowledge* 1542, Andrew Borde counts 'Bryght Helmston' as *"one of the several noble ports and havens to rehearse"* (or resort to). Three years after the publication of Borde's book, D'Annebalte's fleet attacked ships moored at Brighthelmstone. A sketch still exists showing the naval encounter [see below]. By the middle of the seventeenth century, Brighthelmstone had grown to become one of the principal towns of Sussex, containing 600 households, but even then the sea was taking its toll. On one occasion it is recorded that a tenant had eight acres of land washed away in one storm. In the years 1703 and 1705 major storms wreaked havoc to the town, and in the 1738 edition of *Magna Britannia* we read *"The greatest damage to the buildings has been done by the breaking in of the sea, which, within these forty years, has laid waste above 130 tenements; which loss, by modest computation, amounts to near 40,000; and if some speedy care is not taken to stop the en croachments of the ocean, it is probable that the town will be in a few years utterly depopulated, the inhabitants already being diminished one-third less than they were."*

In November 1723, one of the many disastrous inunda tions had occurred. A large vessel was swept into the pool at Brighthelmstone, and much damage was caused by it. By the middle of the eighteenth century, the old town had been com pletely abandoned. Encroachment of the sea had forced land owners and tenants to build a new town further inland, laying the foundations of modern Brighton. The area later occupied by Brighton's Ship Street and Black Lion Street was formerly to the north of Brighthelmstone, being known as The Hempshires, where gardens had been laid out for the cultivation of hemp for rope-making and other purposes. This area was built over as Brighthelmstone perished.

66. The 'Daddy Longlegs' was a mobile Victorian pier on rails that ran on the foreshore at Brighton. It was damaged by the sea a few days after it began operation, and was eventually sold for scrap.

Erosion in the Brighton area has always been spectacularly rapid. In the reign of Henry ll, the road which connected Rottingdean and Brighthelmstone was nearly a mile from the sea's edge, but by the beginning of the nineteenth century, it was teetering on the cliff edge, and a new highway, which nowadays itself runs close to the cliffs edge, had to be cut some way to the north of the old road. The old road, needless to say, has long since gone 'down the cliff'. ln the *Brighton Guardian* of June 18th, 1876, some measure of the rate of coastal attrition then taking place was given by Henry Willett. "*Some of your readers will be startled to know,*" wrote Willett, "*that the progressive en croachments of the sea opposite the new gas-works at Aldrington* (about three miles west of Brighton) *obtained by actual measurement, has been in the last ten years 270 feet, or at an annual rate of nine yards... A good mile further along the beach I arrived at Brighthemstead, a large, ill-built, irregular market-town, mostly inhabited with sea-faring men. This town is likely to share the same fate as the last, the sea having washed away the half of it; whole streets being now deserted, and the beach almost covered with walls of houses being almost entire, the lime or cement being strong enough when thrown down to resist the violence of the waves.*"

Of Hove, *Magna Britannica* writes "*This place was a considerable village long after the Norman times, but it is now almost entirely swallowed up by the sea.*" Further up the coast is Shoreham, which has also suffered erosive depredations. One of the principal English seaports in the reign of Edward III, building and manning more ships than Boston, Bristol, Dover or Hull, Shoreham was so badly attacked by the sea that by 1432 it possessed only 36 inhabitants. By the sixteenth century, Camden could write: "*Somewhere lower upon the shore appeareth Shoreham, also being drowned and made even with the sea, is no more to be seene...*"

On the Sussex coast, as on the coast of Norfolk, Holderness and Wales, the orientation of roads gives a good clue to the sites of former habitation. In the area around the Norfolk villages of Winterton and Sea Palling, to travel northwards, one must drive along roads which are composed of a continuing series of 'dogs legs'. These roads are merely connecting links between the once far more important roads running inland from the coast.

The villages and towns formerly served by these roads have long since been swallowed by the sea, and in general they remain as tracks running through fields towards the sand-dune covered sea defences. In Norfolk, the only places they remain important roads is where they serve as access to the summertime holiday beaches, as at Caister and Sea Palling. In Sussex, the roads around Aldwick, Great Bognor and Ancton also run to dead ends. They, too, formerly served as access to lost towns - Charlton llsham, Cudlowe and two other settlements whose names have disappeared in the mists of history.

Selsey

Although Selsey today is no more than an unremarkable coastal town and promontory, a mile from the present shore once stood an important and commanding sacred place - Selsey Cathedral. The first monastery founded in Sussex, this shrine was set up by the celebrated St Wilfrid in AD 680, who was its first bishop. The monastery remained an episcopal see for 400 years, with an unbroken succession of bishops officiating from the great Saxon minster. The design and precise positioning of this great building is not known, but it is recorded that landward from the cathedral and its adjoining bishop's palace stretched a forest known as Selsey Wood. Thousands of acres in extent, Selsey Wood was stocked with many deer and other choice game, but all that remains now of the hunting forest is a piece of sea designated "The Park", formerly an important anchorage for fishing vessels. Although the cathedral was demolished in Norman times, the Park continued with game until the early seventeenth century, the see having gone to Chichester in 1075.

Selsey and its Park were held in great sanctity, for it was an offense punishable by an official church curse and excommunication to poach the deer. As late as the sixteenth century, Bishop Rede, whose habitation was by then the nearby Amberley

Castle, issued a curse against poachers to be read in every church in the deanery. This must remain conjecture, for by the time of Camden the ruins of Selsey Cathedral were only visible at low tide. *'In this isle remaineth only the dead carkases as it were,"* he wrote *"of that ancient little citie, wherein those bishops sate, and the same hidden quite with water at everie tide, but at low water evident and plaine to be seen."* Various stones have been dredged from the sea bed at the site of the Saxon cathedral, and its associated lore includes the ubiquitous 'spectral bells' motif. As late as the 1930s, Selsey was estimated to be still losing six feet of land a year to the incessant hunger of the waves.

Sussex has suffered more than most counties in the uneven battle with the sea. The *Taxatio Ecclesiastica*, compiled in 1292, and *Nonarum Inquisitions in Curia Saccani* (1340), contains many entries recording coastal losses. Between the years 1260 and 1340, the following losses took place in Selsey Brighton district: *"Selseye, much arable land; Felpham, 60 acres; Brighthelmston, 40 acres; Aldington, 40 acres; Portslade, 60 acres; Lancing, much land; Hove, 150 acres; and Heas, 400 acres."* These figures mean more than mere loss of land to the sea; in many cases they represented the loss of livelihood or the ruination of families or even whole communities, for in the Middle Ages there was no insurance cover, and little enough disaster relief. Once a house and its surrounding land was destroyed by the sea, its owner was utterly destitute.

Isle of Wight

We have seen already how some islands around our coast were formerly connected; Priestholm and Hilbre are two famous examples. But it is not commonly realised that the Isle of Wight was still connected to mainland Britain within historic times. Until the eighteenth century, the Isle of Wight was cut off from the rest of Britain only at high tide, being accessible across the sands at other times. Worsley, the Isle of Wight's historian, noted that a hard gravelly beach extends a great way across the channel at the extremity where the tides meet. An ancient road known as Rue Street runs across the island towards this narrow point, showing the characteristics of those roads in other parts of the country whose purpose was to serve towns now inundated by the sea. In the case of Rue Street, its function was most probably access with the mainland via the point of Hampshire known as The Leap. it is difficult to imagine another use for this road, for Beckles Willson, writing in 1901 could assert "Many parts of this road are of little or no use at this time." Erosion around the coast of the Isle of Wight has certainly been severe as attested by spectacular cliff formations like the famous Needles.

Back on the mainland, the coast between Hurst Point and Christchurch has also suffered attrition, and has consequently retreated a considerable distance. At Portland and Purbeck there are several accounts of massive cliff falls being occasioned by severe storms. In 1665, a portion of cliff adjoining the quarries fell into the sea. It was over a hundred yards wide. In 1734 a fall of over fifty yards occurred on the east side of the isle, but in 1792 was the largest collapse on record, when a landslip of gargantuan proportions moved an area of ground 600 yards from east to west and over a mile and a quarter from north to south in one massive slip towards the sea.

Axmouth

Massive slips of this nature have long been the norm on the cliff s around Axmouth in south-east Devon. Over the years, they have produced a spectacular geological formation that has long been the object of study by geographers and geologists. Various major collapses are documented in this region, which stretches from the mouth of the River Axe, near Culverhole Point, to the county boundary at Devonshire Head, by Lyme Regis. For about four miles, there is a series of collapsed blocks stretching about a quarter of a mile wide between the sea and a line of inland cliffs. At Dowland and Bindon, a vast chasm isolates a section of land from the main cliff.

One of the major cliff-falls in recent history took place in the year 1839, after a year of abnormal rainfall and exceptional gales. On December 23rd of that year, fissures were noticed opening in the cliffs belonging to Dowlands Farm, but not sufficiently to cause undue alarm. At one o'clock in the morning of Christmas Day, 1839, a man named Critchard was returning home from the ancient Yule ceremony of burning the ashen faggot at Dowlands Farm when he noticed that the path into the undercliff had sunk, and that his cottage was even deeper. At about four in the morning, Critchard heard a "wonderful crack" and about an hour later he had difficulty in opening the door. By that time the roof beams were settling, and fissures had appeared in the cottage garden. He woke his neighbours and they carried out as many possessions as they could. Critchard scrambled up the rapidly-subsiding path to the farm for help, and a cart was sent down to pick up the labourers' belonging. By the time the cart returned, the road was badly fissured, and had to be re-made in places before the cart could proceed. Before long, Critchard's cottage had been twisted out of shape, and another, which stood to the west of it, completely razed.

The next night, a strong gale was blowing. Two coastguards were going about their duty when one tripped over a ridge of gravel near the clifftop of Dowlands. The ridge had not been there the night before. One of them stumbled into a fissure, trapping his leg. By moonlight they saw fissures opening up all around them and heard a great tearing sound. Freeing his trapped leg, the coastguard rejoined his companion and they hastily beat a retreat to their station at Whitlands. Two other men who were near Culverhole Point noticed a great heaving of the beach, and saw the sea becoming violently agitated as a dark ridge rose in the water. They were terrified by the cliffs falling all around them, accompanied by *"flashes of fire, and a strong smell of sulphur."*

Between Christmas Eve, when the subsidences or earthquakes began, and Boxing Day, over 150 million cubic feet of material collapsed, an estimated eight million tons of disrupted rock, destroying an area of twenty acres. The fields on the clifftop had moved bodily towards the sea, but the hedges forming the fields' boundaries remained unharmed, having shifted between 200 and 400 feet seaward.

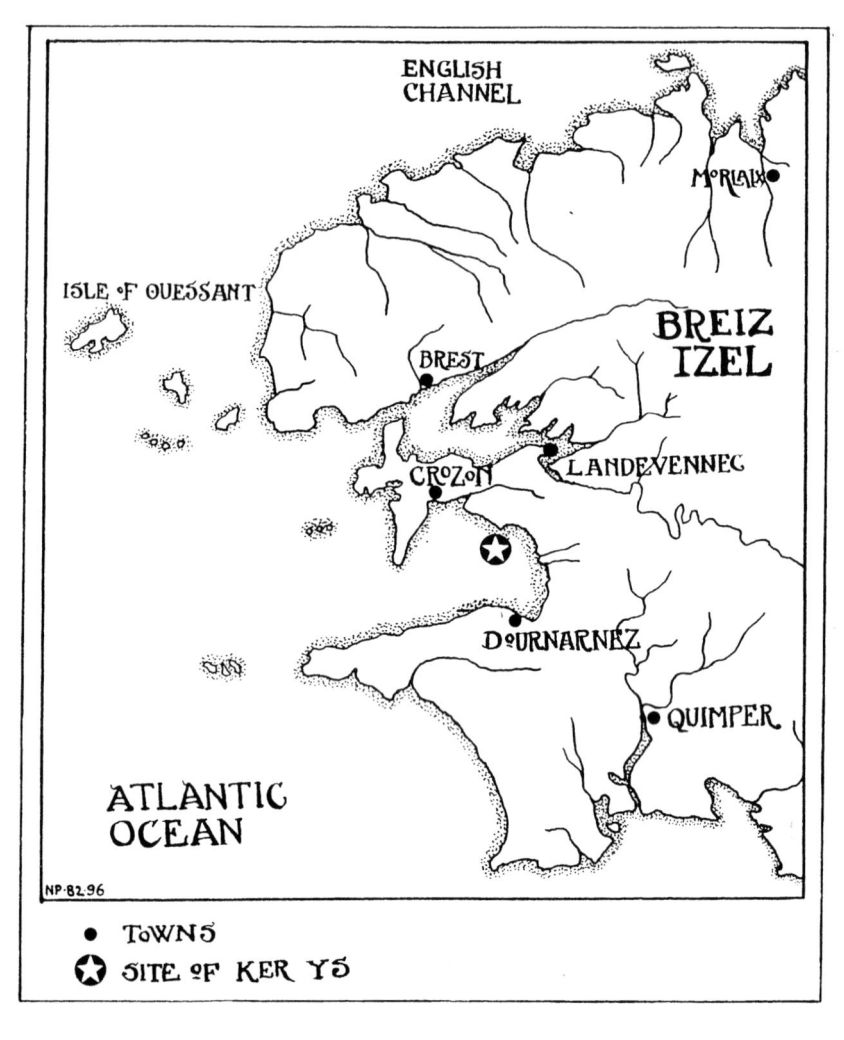

67. Map of Brittany, showing the location of the lost town of Ker Ys.

This catastrophe naturally attracted the attention of scientist and crank alike, and many eminent geologists visited the place to describe the unprecedented events in their learned tracts. The landslip also caused a London apocalyptic to produce a pamphlet titled in the verbose manner of the times *A Brief Account of the Earthquake, the Solemn Euent which Occurred near Axmouth*. This tract proved "*beyond all doubt*" that the event was a fulfilment of a prophecy in the Revelation of St John the Divine, and that the end was nigh."

A Breton Legend

One of the most famous lost towns in Celtic mythology is the Breton town of Ker Ys, which stood in the place now occupied by the Bay of Douarnenez, Finisterre. Traditionally, Ys was destroyed at the same time period ascribed to the inundation of Lyonesse and the Welsh lost lands. It is immortalised in an old Breton poem which recounts the sad tale of Ys, and its king, Gradlon:

> *Didst thou hear what Guenole said to king Gradlon*
> *whose residence is at Ker Ys?*
> *"Here lust prevails; here all vices have their sway.*
> *Tremble you all! As sorrow treads on the steps of*
> *pleasure!*
> *Whoever bites into the forbidden fruit shall be bitten too*
> *By that forbidden fruit and whoever laughs too much*
> *shall one day cry!"*
> *Dahut, the only daughter of Gradlon, wanton Dahut,*
> *laughs and dances and mocks the holy monk.*
>
> *In the King's palace, a thousand torches are ablaze.*
> *Pipers are playing their finest tunes.*
> *Men and women are eating and drinking overmuch, to*
> *the sound of the bagpipes.*

68. The escape of King Gradlon.

*Through the great gates, an unknown gentleman has
   slipped; dressed in red, in red from his feet up to
   his head.*
The red horseman has sat near Dahut.

Gradlon spake thus:
"Noble friends, I shall withdraw and sleep a little.
*You will sleep tomorrow morning; stay with us tonight;
   however, do as you choose, if it pleases you."*
*Thereupon, the red horseman dances with Dahut; he
   softly whispers into the Princess's ear:*
*"Fair Dahut, I will love thee on the dam, to the sound of
   the waves,*
Take the key, it will be a fine sight!"

*Now, whoever had seen Gradlon in his sleep would have
   felt respect- Respect, when seeing him in his
   purple bed, with his snow-white hair*
On his shoulders, his golden chain around his neck.
*Whoever had been on watch would have seen the white
   girl*
*Softly enter the room in her bare feet, crawl to the king,
   her father*
And carry off the chain and key to the dams.

*The king is still asleep, the old king; and a cry suddenly
   goes up through the night:*
"Water is Coming in!"
King, rise from thy bed; to horse! and fly far from here.
*Cursed be Dahut, the white girl, who, after the feast,
   opened the gates of the dams of Ker Ys!*

*Gradlon mounts his horse; he flies away through the
   darness;*
*He hears the clamour of dying men and the crash of his
   crumbling town.*

The monk then arrives on a black charger.
Over the water he flies, like a seagull.

69. St Guenolé, image at Kernuz, Brittany.

> "King, throw far from thee the demon that thou carryest,
> or else thou art lose!"
> Gradlon feels that his heart breaks within him, and
> hesitates.
>
> *The sea opens its abysses and Dahut is swallowed up by*
> *the deep.*
> *The king's horse, now lighter, reaches the shore.*
> *Dahut, since then, is calling sailors to be wrecked.*

The Ys tale encapsulated all of the themes found associated with lost towns around the British coast; the wanton licentious court, the warning; the drunken opening of the sea-gates; and the flight on horseback. Even the post-cataclysm sounds from the sea are mentioned. The saint who warned Gradlon of the impending doom of Ys is Winwaloe, here spelt with its French version as Guenole. Like many saints of his period, Winwaloe has many alternative spellings, but probably holds the record with fifty recorded versions. Although born in Brittany, Winwaloe was the son of Fracan, cousin of Cado, Duke of Kernow (Cornwall). Winwaloe's date of birth is commonly stated to be the year 457 AD. His connection with the inundation of Ys, and thus by implication the control of tidal matters is strengthened by an incident from his early life.

Having become the leading Christian preacher in his part of the country, Winwaloe set up a monastery on the island of Thopepigia, in what is now Brest Harbour. Although his monastery was a success, and the community flourished there for three years, after mature deliberation the monk decided that he and his small Christian band should move on. Taking the hand of a disciple, and forming a human chain, Winwaloe boldly strode into the sea to walk towards the land. The tide, so the story goes, receded miraculously before the holy man, and the monks proceeded dryshod to the shore, when previously they had been forced to use a boat. Miracle over, the saint selected a new site for his monastery - the celebrated Breton shrine of Landevennec. It is a strange coincidence that two major events in the saint's life should be connected with fluctuations of the sea, and though

70. Sculpture of King Gradlon on Quimper Cathedral.

the Breton tradition does not state it, it is probable that earlier traditions ascribed the cause of the inundation of Ys to Winwaloe's personal power.

Postscript

In the days before nuclear holocaust was seen as the probable end of the world, many soothsayers and astrologers forecast a universal flood as the final act. Sometimes, people took them seriously. In 1524, the German astrologer Stoffler predicted that a major inundation was imminent. Taking Stoffler's prognostications at face value, Doctor Auriol of Toulouse proceeded to build a magnificent ark large enough not only for himself and his immediate family, but also for his close friends. Of course, the good doctor was the laughing-stock of Toulouse when the expected deluge did not materialise.

The awesome power of great masses of water can never be controlled by human action; it is on a literally cosmic scale, bound up with gravitation of extraterrestrial bodies. Since time immemorial, this unstoppable force has been naturally ascribed to the gods, or in monotheistic religions to the supreme unitary deity. When areas have been obliterated, the deluge has been seen as the wrath of heaven unleashed against unheeding and unrepentant sinners, object lessons indeed for those who would presume to flout divine law. But in a less religious age, these forces are seen as manifestations of the blind forces of the universe, to be controlled by those who possess sufficient knowhow It is an ever-present human desire to attempt to avoid or at least postpone, the inevitable, not least in the realms of coastal losses. Because of this, research still continues into the subtle conditions that affect coastal changes.

New sea defences are continually being erected, as old ones are patched up for a few more years' service. A barrage has recently been constructed at Woolwich to prevent the predicted flooding of London. It may well serve for several centuries hence, but finally the continuous subsidence of south-eastern England will produce the condi tions for London to be overwhelmed. Then, like Vineta,

Thule, Hy-Brasil and Atlantis, London will join the roll-call of lost cities, receding first into history and finally, into the unimaginably distant future of mythology.

Bibliography

Aitchison, George: *Unknown Brighton*, London 1926.
Ashton, W.: *The Evolution of a Coastline*, London 1920
Benoit, Pierre: *Atlantida*, Paris.
Borde, Andrew: *The Book of Knowledge*, London I 542.
Boyle. J.R.: *Lost Towns of the Humber*, Kingston-upon-hull, 1889.
Brown, Jerry Earl: *Under the City of the Angels*, New York, 1981.
Camden, William: *Britannia*, various editions.
Collis, W.: *Lectures on Sewers*, London,1622.
Cooper, W.D.: *The History of Winchelsea*, London, 1850.
Croker, T.C.: *Fairy Legends of the South of Ireland*, London, 1828.
de La Beche, Henry: *The Report on Cornwall*
Dockwra, Sir Henry: *Memories of the Tyrone Rebellion*, London.
Donnelly, Ignatius: *Atlantis. the Antediluvian World*, London, 1948.
Dugdale, W.: *The History of Embanking*
Edwards, Mr.: *The Survey of the Witham*, 1769.
Edwards, Griffith: *The Inundation of Cantre'r Gwaelod, or the lowland Hundred*, Tenby, 1849.
Gould, S. Baring: *Cunous Myths of the Middle Ages*, London, 1894.
Gray, Thomas.: *The Buried City of Kenfig*, London, 1909.
Hardisson Stein: *Olafs Drapa*, 11th cent.
Harland, M.G. and H.J.: *The Flooding of Eastern England*. Peterborough, 1980.
Harrison, F. and North, J.S.: *Old Brighton, Old Houe, Old Preston*, London, 1937.
Heimreich, A.: *Nordfresische Chronika*, 1666.
Howells, W.: *Cambrian Superstitions*, Tipton, 1831.
Hunt, B.P. Stather: *Flinten History*, Lowestoft, 1953.
Jones, Owen, et. al.: *The Myrvyrian Archaeology of Wales*, London 1801-7.
Kirfel, W.: *Die Cosmographie der Inder*, Bonn 1920.
Lucian: *De Deae Syrias*, BC 170.
Lyell. Sir Charles: *Principles of Geology*.2 vols. London, 1867.
Merlin: *The Prophecies*, various editions.
Meyrick, S.R.: *The History and Antiquities of the County of Cardiganshire*, Brecon, 1808.
Monmouth, Geoffrey of: *The History of the Kings of Britain*
Muck, Otto: *The Secret of Atlantis*. London, 1978.
North, F.J.: *The Evolution of the Bristol Channel*, Cardiff, 1955.
- - - *Sunken Cities* Cardiff, 1957,
Perry, Capt. *An account of the Stopping of Daggenham Breach* 1721.
Pugh, Edward: *Cambna Depicta*, 1816.
Ray, John: *Itinerary* 1662.
Rees, Rice: *Essay on the Welsh Saints*.
Rhys J.: *Celtic Britain*, London,1904.

Roberts, Anthony: *Atlantean Traditions in Ancient Britain*, Llanfynydd, 1974.
Roberts, H.A.E.: *Legends and Folklore of North Wales*, London, 1931.
Scott-Elliot, J.: *The Story of Atlantis*, London, 1896.
Shakespeare, William: *Richard II*.
- *King Lear*.
- *Sonnets*.
Short, Thomas: *A General Chronolgical History of the Air. Weather. Seasons, Meteors Etc...* London, 1749.
Skene, W.F.: *The Four Ancient Books of Wales*, Edinburgh, 1868.
Steers, J.A.: *The Coastline of England and Wales*, Cambridge, 1948.
Sturluson Snorri: *Heimsknngla*, Iceland, 1177.
Teudt, Wilhelm: *Germanische Heiligtumer*, Jena, 1929.
Thomas, Charles: *Exploration of a drowned landscape: Archaeology and history of the Isles of Scilly*. London, 1985
Thomas, W. Jenkyn: *The Welsh Fairy Book*, Cardiff, 1952.
Thornber, W.: *Historical and Descriptive Account of Blackpool*, Blackpool, 1837.
Thucydides: *The Peloponnesian Wars*, (circa BC 420).
Walters, Cuming: *Bygone Suffolk*, London, 1901.
Webb, William: *The King's Vale Royal*.
Weaver: *Ancient Funeral Monuments*, London, 1631.
White: *The Directory of Suffolk*, 1844.
Williams, ab Ithel, J.: *Brut y Tywysogion*, London, 1860.
Williams William: *The History of Beaumaris*, 1669.
Willson, Henry Beckles: *The Story of Lost England*, London, 1902.
Wirth, Hermann: *Die Heilige Urschrift der Menschheit*, Leipzig, 1932-6.
Wood, Anthony: *Athenae Oxonienses*, Oxford 1691-2.
Virgil: *The Aenid*.

Journals - Reports Consulted

Antiquity; Archaeologia; Archaeologia Cambrensis; The Brighton Guardian; Y Brython; The Cambrian Quarterly Magazine and Celtic Repository; The Cambrian Register; Collins's Hydrographic Survey; The Field; Folklore; The Gentleman's Magazine; The Grimsby Telegraph; The Hull and East Riding Portfolio; Institute of Oceanographic Sciences Reports; The Liverpool Courier; The Lynn News and Advertiser; Megalithic Visions Antiquarian Papers; Ordnance Survey Profes sional Papers, Series 4.; Proceedings of the Chester Arch2010gical Society; Proceedings of the Geological Society of London; Proceedings of the Liverpool Geological Society; Quarterly Journal of the Geological Society; The Royal Commission on Coast Erosion and the Reclamation of Tidal Lands, 1907.; Sussex Archaeological Collections; Transactions of the Cardiff Antiquarian Society; Transactions of The Historic Society of Lancashire and Cheshire; Transactions of the Honourable Society of Cymmrodorion; Transactions of the Institute of British Geographers; Welsh Outlook; Y Traethodydd.

Traditional Sources

The Bible; The Edda: The Koran; The Popol Vuh; The Rig Veda; The Zend Avesta.

FREE DETAILED CATALOGUE

A detailed illustrated catalogue is available on request, SAE or International Postal Coupon appreciated. Titles are available direct from Capall Bann, post free in the UK (cheque or PO with order) or from good bookshops and specialist outlets. Titles currently available include:

Animals, Mind Body Spirit & Folklore
Angels and Goddesses - Celtic Christianity & Paganism by Michael Howard
Arthur - The Legend Unveiled by C Johnson & E Lung
Auguries and Omens - The Magical Lore of Birds by Yvonne Aburrow
Book of the Veil The by Peter Paddon
Caer Sidhe - Celtic Astrology and Astronomy by Michael Bayley
Call of the Horned Piper by Nigel Jackson
Cats' Company by Ann Walker
Celtic Lore & Druidic Ritual by Rhiannon Ryall
Compleat Vampyre - The Vampyre Shaman: Werewolves & Witchery by Nigel Jackson
Crystal Clear - A Guide to Quartz Crystal by Jennifer Dent
Earth Dance - A Year of Pagan Rituals by Jan Brodie
Earth Harmony - Places of Power, Holiness and Healing by Nigel Pennick
Earth Magic by Margaret McArthur
Enchanted Forest - The Magical Lore of Trees by Yvonne Aburrow
Familiars - Animal Powers of Britain by Anna Franklin
Healing Homes by Jennifer Dent
Herbcraft - Shamanic & Ritual Use of Herbs by Susan Lavender & Anna Franklin
In Search of Herne the Hunter by Eric Fitch
Inner Space Workbook - Developing Counselling & Magical Skills Through the Tarot
Kecks, Keddles & Kesh by Michael Bayley
Living Tarot by Ann Walker
Magical Incenses and Perfumes by Jan Brodie
Magical Lore of Cats by Marion Davies
Magical Lore of Herbs by Marion Davies
Masks of Misrule - The Horned God & His Cult in Europe by Nigel Jackson
Mysteries of the Runes by Michael Howard
Oracle of Geomancy by Nigel Pennick
Patchwork of Magic by Julia Day
Pathworking - A Practical Book of Guided Meditations by Pete Jennings
Pickingill Papers - The Origins of Gardnerian Wicca by Michael Howard
Psychic Animals by Dennis Bardens
Psychic Self Defence - Real Solutions by Jan Brodie
Runic Astrology by Nigel Pennick
Sacred Animals by Gordon MacLellan
Sacred Grove - The Mysteries of the Forest by Yvonne Aburrow
Sacred Geometry by Nigel Pennick
Sacred Lore of Horses The by Marion Davies
Sacred Ring - Pagan Origins British Folk Festivals & Customs by Michael Howard
Seasonal Magic - Diary of a Village Witch by Paddy Slade
Secret Places of the Goddess by Philip Heselton
Talking to the Earth by Gordon Maclellan
Taming the Wolf - Full Moon Meditations by Steve Hounsome
The Goddess Year by Nigel Pennick & Helen Field
West Country Wicca by Rhiannon Ryall
Witches of Oz The by Matthew & Julia Phillips

Capall Bann is owned and run by people actively involved in many of the areas in which we publish. Our list is expanding rapidly so do contact us for details on the latest releases.

Capall Bann Publishing, Freshfields, Chieveley, Berks, RG20 8TF